Draw THE SEASHORE

Martin Ursell

Series Editors: David and Brenda Herbert

A & C BLACK · LONDON

Reissued in 1990
First published 1982
A & C Black (Publishers) Limited
35 Bedford Row, London WC1R 4JH

ISBN 0-7136-3297-6

Printed and bound in Great Britain by
Hollen Street Press Ltd, Slough, Berkshire

Contents

Making a start 4

What to draw with 6

What to draw on 8

Perspective 10

Masses and planes 13

Building up a drawing
1 Pebbles 14
2 Crabs 16
3 Shells 18

Structure and pattern
1 Shells 20
2 Sand and shingle 22

Quick sketches on the spot 24

More careful drawing
Fish 30
Seaweed 34

Same subject, different media 36

Collecting 38

Water 44

The longer view 46

Making a start

Learning to draw is largely a matter of practice and observation — so draw as much and as often as you can, and use your eyes all the time.

The seashore is a marvellous place to draw. There is an enormous variety of subject-matter — rocks, water, marine life, birds, and all kinds of objects such as shells, pebbles, driftwood, seaweed and things washed up by the tide, many of which can be taken home to be studied in detail.

Carry a sketchbook with you whenever possible, and don't be shy of using it in public, either for quick notes to be used later or for a finished drawing. The time you spend on a drawing is not important. A ten-minute sketch can say more than a slow, painstaking drawing that takes many hours.

To do an interesting drawing, you must enjoy it. Even if you start on something that doesn't particularly interest you, you will probably find that the act of drawing it — and looking at it in a new way — creates its own excitement. The less you think about how you are drawing and the more you think about what you are drawing, the better your drawing will be.

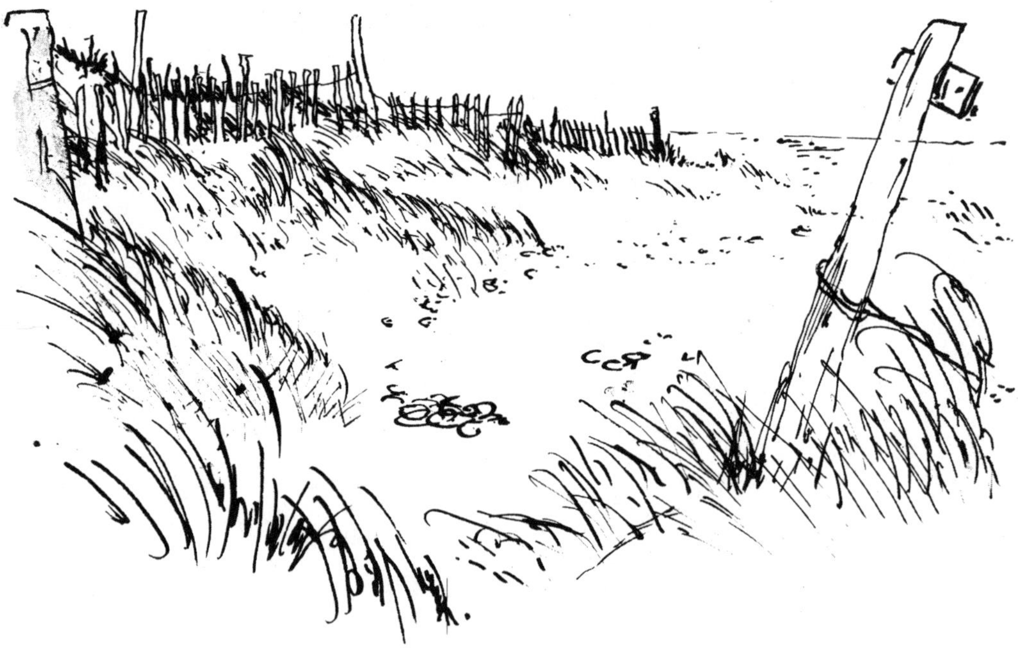

The best equipment will not itself make you a better artist — a masterpiece can be drawn with a stump of pencil on a scrap of paper. But good equipment is encouraging and pleasant to use, so buy the best you can afford and don't be afraid to use it freely.

Be as bold as you dare. It's your piece of paper and you can do what you like with it. Experiment with the biggest piece of paper and the boldest, softest piece of chalk or crayon you can find, filling the paper with lines — scribbles, lettering, anything — to get a feeling of freedom. Even if you think you have a gift for tiny delicate line drawings with a fine pen or pencil, this is worth trying. It will act as a 'loosening up' exercise. The results may surprise you.

Be self-critical. If a drawing looks wrong, scrap it and start again. A second, third or even fourth attempt will often be better than the first, because you are learning more about the subject all the time. Use an eraser as little as possible — piecemeal correction won't help. Don't re-trace your lines. If a line is right the first time, leave it alone — heavier re-drawing leads to a dull, mechanical look.

You can learn a certain amount from looking at other people's drawings. But you will learn more from a drawing done from direct observation of the subject or even out of your head, however stiff and unsatisfactory the results may seem at first.

A lot can be learned by practice and from books, but a teacher can be a great help. If you get the chance, don't hesitate to join a class — even one evening a week can do a lot of good.

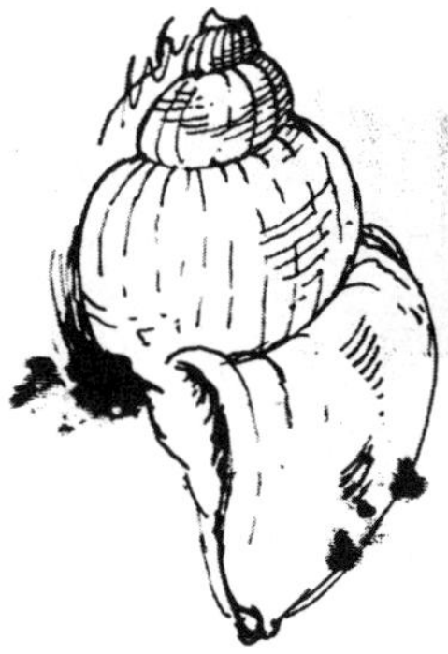

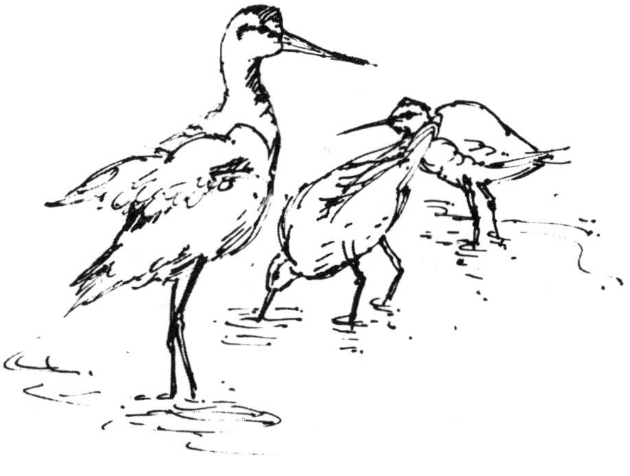

What to draw with

Pencils are graded according to hardness, from 6H (the hardest) through 5H, 4H, 3H, 2H to H; then HB; then B, through 1B, 2B, 3B, 4B, 5B up to 6B (the softest). For most purposes, a soft pencil (HB or softer) is best. If you keep it sharp, it will draw as fine a line as a hard pencil but with less pressure, which makes it easier to control. Sometimes it is effective to smudge the line with your finger or an eraser, but if you do this too much the drawing will look woolly. A fine range of graphite drawing pencils is Royal Sovereign.

Charcoal (which is very soft) is excellent for large, bold sketches, but not for detail. Beware of accidental smudging: a drawing can even be dusted or rubbed off the paper altogether. To prevent this spray with fixative. Charcoal pencils, such as the Royal Sovereign, are also very useful.

Wax crayons (also soft) are not easily smudged or erased. You can scrape a line away from a drawing on good quality paper, or partly scrape a drawing to get special effects.

Oil pastels, marker pencils, chinagraph and lithographic chalk are similar to wax crayons.

Conté crayons, wood-cased or in solid sticks, are available in various degrees of hardness, and in several colours. The cased crayons are easy to sharpen, but the solid sticks are more fun — you can use the side of the stick for large areas of tone. Conté is harder than charcoal, but it is also easy to smudge. The black is very intense.

Pastels (available in a wide range of colours) are softer still. Since drawings in pastel are usually called 'paintings', they are really beyond the scope of this book.

Pens vary as much as pencils or crayons. Ink has a quality of its own, but of course it cannot be erased. Mapping pens are only suitable for delicate detail and minute cross-hatching.

Special artists' pens, such as Gillott 303 and Gillott 404 allow you a more varied line, according to the angle at which you hold them and the pressure you use. The Gillott 659 is a very popular crowquill pen.

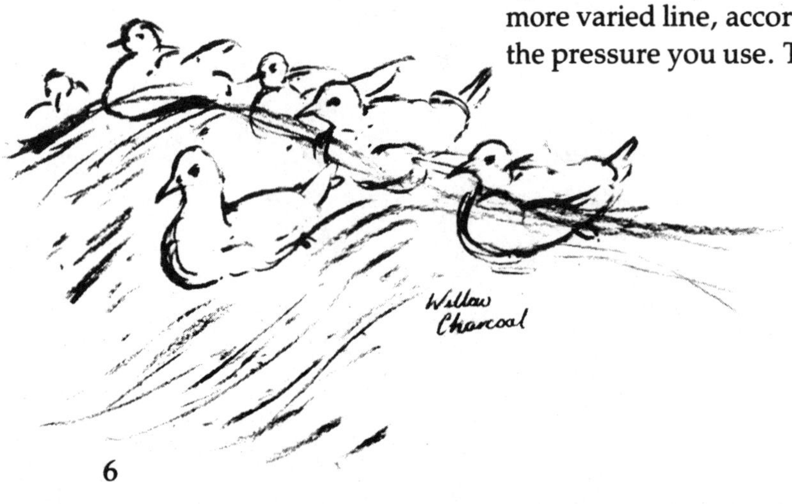

Reed, bamboo and quill pens are good for bold lines and you can make the nib end narrower or wider with the help of a sharp knife or razor blade. This kind of pen has to be dipped frequently into the ink.

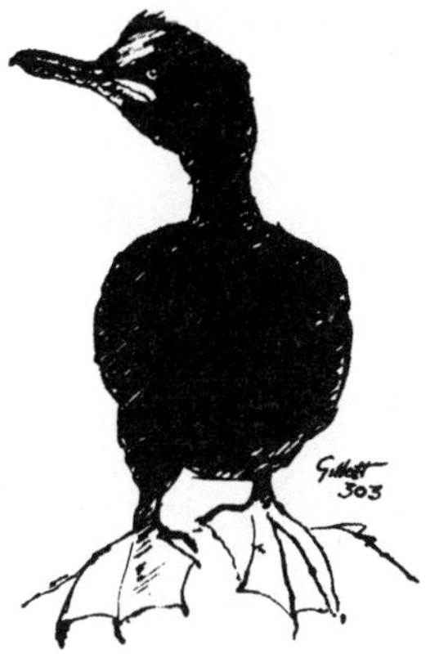

Fountain pens have a softer touch than dip-in pens, and many artists prefer them. The portability of the fountain pen makes it a very useful sketching tool.

Special fountain pens, such as Rapidograph and Rotring, control the flow of ink by means of a needle valve in a fine tube (the nib). Nibs are available in several grades of fineness and are interchangeable. The line they produce is of even thickness, but on coarse paper you can draw an interesting broken line similar to that of a crayon. These pens have to be held at a right-angle to the paper, which is a disadvantage.

Inks also vary. Waterproof Indian ink quickly clogs the pen. Pelikan Fount India, which is nearly as black, flows more smoothly and does not leave a varnishy deposit on the pen. Ordinary fountain-pen or writing inks (black, blue, green or brown) are less opaque, so give a drawing more variety of tone. You can mix water with any ink in order to make it thinner; but if you are using Indian ink, add distilled or rain water, because ordinary water will cause it to curdle.

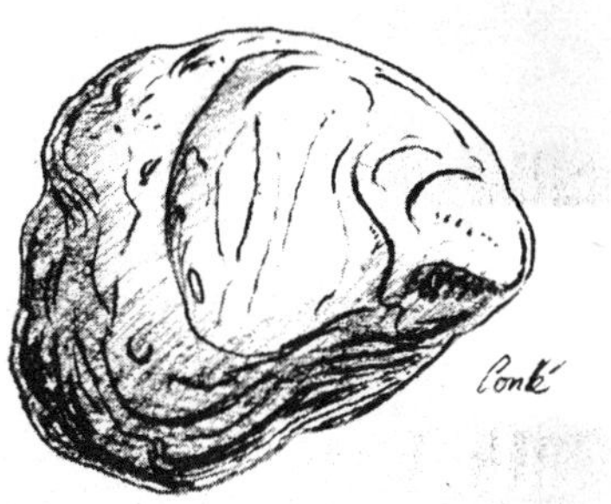

Ball point pens make a drawing look a bit mechanical, but they are cheap and fool-proof and useful for quick notes and scribbles.

Fibre pens are only slightly better, and their points tend to wear down quickly.

Brushes are very versatile drawing instruments. The biggest sable brush has a fine point, and the smallest brush laid on its side provides a line broader than the broadest nib. You can add depth and variety to a pen or crayon drawing by washing over it with a brush dipped in clean water.

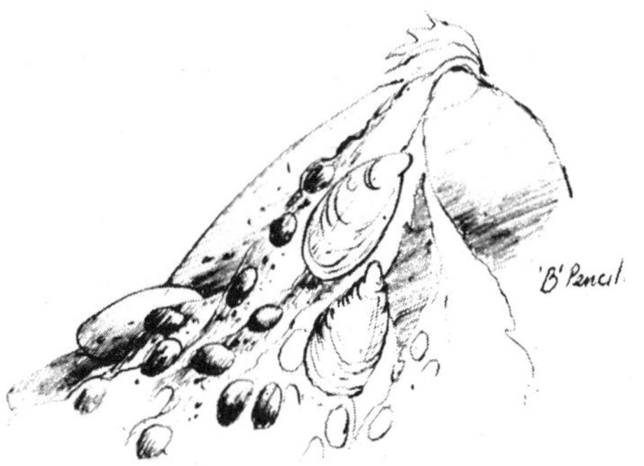

Mixed methods are often pleasing. Try making drawings with pen and pencil, pen and wash or Conté and wash. And try drawing with a pen on wet paper. Pencil and Conté do not look well together and Conté will not draw over pencil or greasy surfaces.

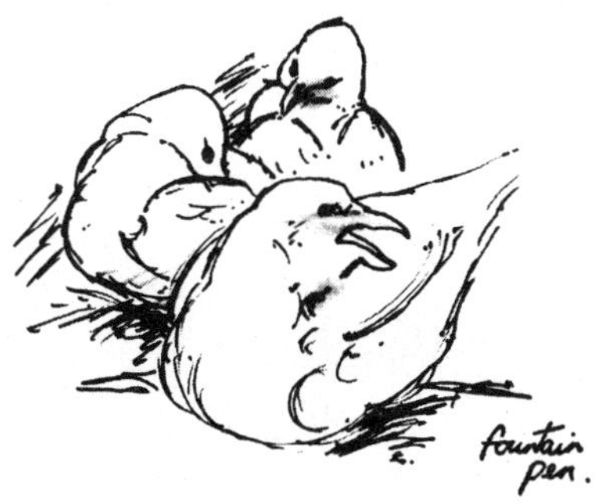

What to draw on

Try as many different surfaces as possible.

Ordinary, inexpensive paper is often as good as anything else: for example, brown and buff wrapping paper (Kraft paper) and lining for wallpaper have surfaces which are particularly suitable for charcoal and soft crayons. Some writing and duplicating papers are best for pen drawings. But there are many papers and brands made specially for the artist.

Bristol board is a smooth, hard white board designed for fine pen work.

Ledger Bond paper (cartridge in the UK), the most usual drawing paper, is available in a variety of surfaces — smooth, 'not surface' (semi-rough), rough.

Watercolour papers also come in various grades of smoothness. They are thick, high-quality papers, expensive but pleasant to use.

Ingres paper is mainly for pastel drawings. It has a soft, furry surface and is made in many light colours — grey, pink, blue, buff, etc.

Sketchbooks, made up from nearly all these papers, are available. Choose one with thin, smooth paper to begin with. Thin paper means more pages, and a smooth surface is best to record detail.

Lay-out pads make useful sketchbooks. Although their covers are not stiff, you can easily insert a stiff piece of card to act as firm backing to your drawing. The paper is semi-transparent, but this can be useful — almost as tracing paper — if you want to make a new, improved version of your last drawing.

An improvised sketchbook can be just as good as a bought one — or better. Find two pieces of thick card, sandwich a stack of paper, preferably of different kinds, between them and clip together at either end.

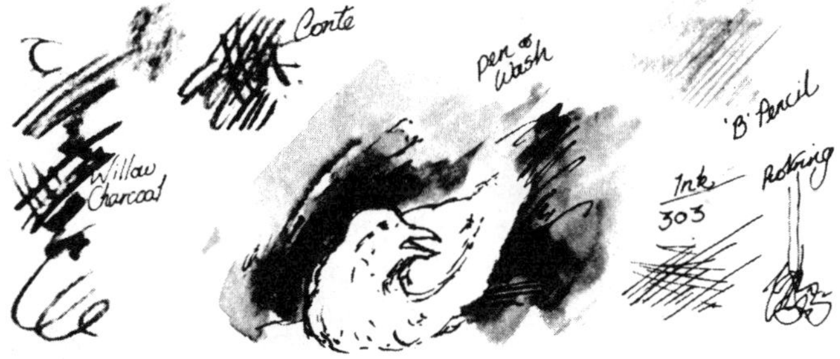

Terston cartidge

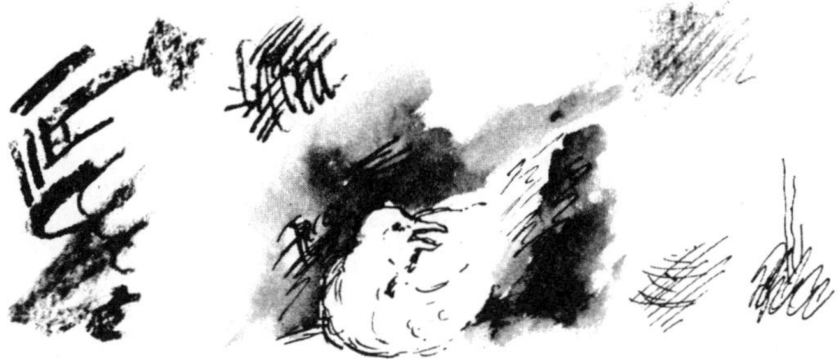

Smooth cartridge

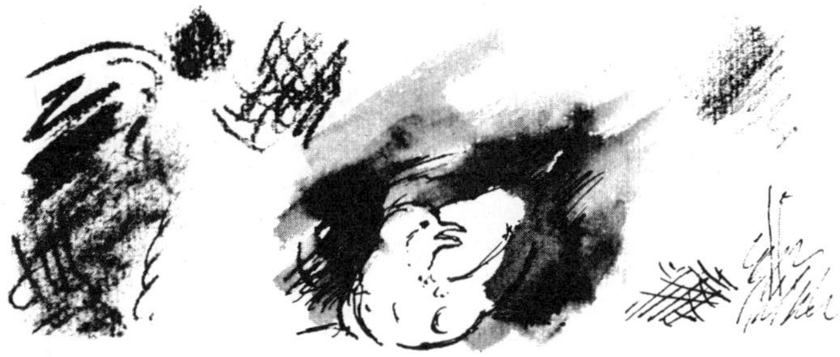

Ingres

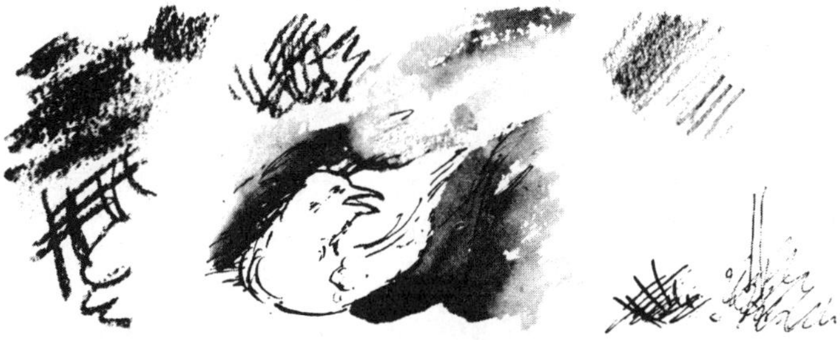

Bockingford watercolour paper

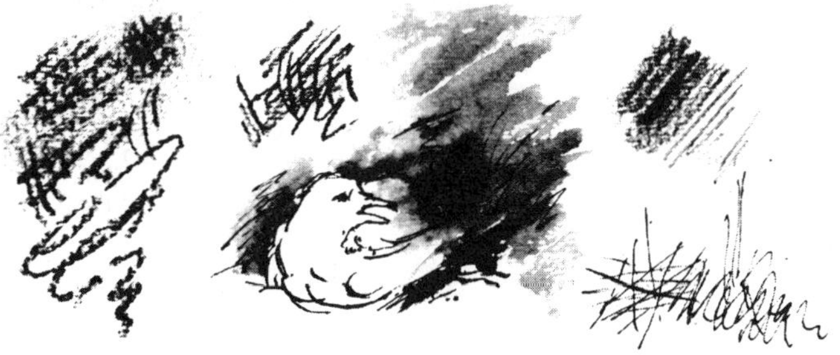

Van Gelder watercolour paper

Perspective

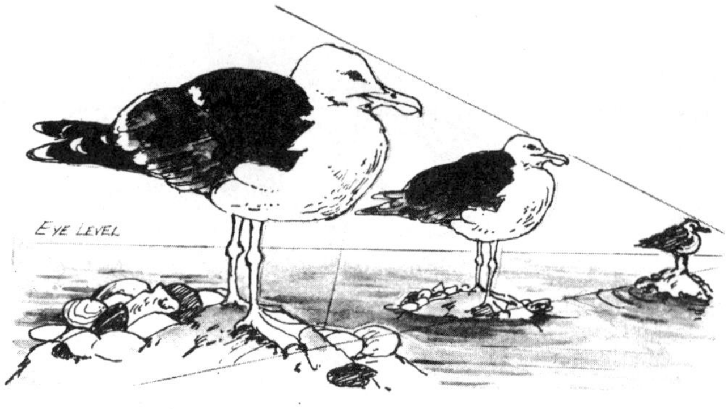

You can be an artist without knowing anything about perspective. Five hundred years ago, when some of the great masterpieces of all time were painted, the word did not even exist. But most beginners want to know something about it in order to make their drawings appear three-dimensional, so here is a short guide.

The further away an object is, the smaller it appears.

All parallel horizontal lines that are directly opposite you, at right-angles to your line of vision, remain parallel.

All horizontal lines that are in fact parallel but go away from you will appear to converge at eye-level at the same vanishing point on the horizon. Lines that are above your eye-level will seem to run downwards towards the vanishing point; lines that are below your eye-level will run upwards. (Look at the drawing on page 12.) You can check the angles of these lines against a pencil held horizontally at eye-level.

The larger and closer any object is, the bigger the front of it will seem to be in relation to the part furthest away, or to any other more distant object. Its actual shape will appear foreshortened or distorted.

If the side of an object is facing you, one vanishing point is enough; but if the corner is facing you, as in the drawing of the beach hut, two vanishing points will be needed.

It may even be necessary to use three vanishing points when your eye is well above or below an object, but these occasions are rare.

Diagonal lines drawn between the opposite angles of a square or rectangle will meet at a point which is half-way along its length or breadth. This remains true when the square or rectangle is foreshortened.

When drawing a circular shape, the following is useful: a circle drawn inside a square will touch the square at the centre point of each of its sides. A foreshortened circle will turn into an oval, but will still touch the centre points of each side of a similarly foreshortened square. However distorted the square, the circle will remain a true oval but will seem to tilt as the square moves to left or right of the vanishing point. The same is true of half circles.

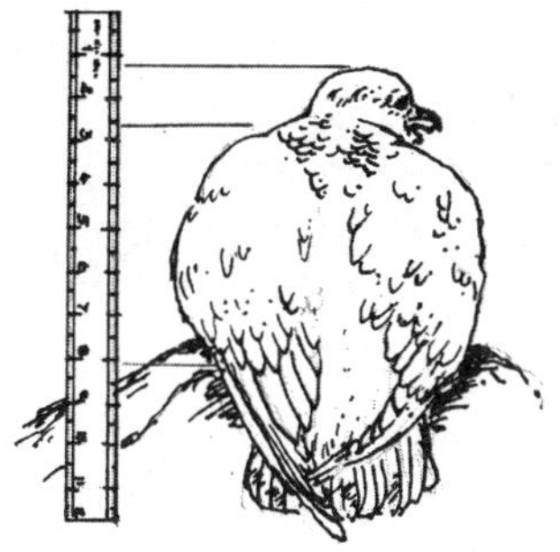

You will tend to exaggerate the apparent depth of top surfaces because you know the shape they really are and want to show this in your drawing. You can check the correct apparent depth of any foreshortened receding plane by using a pencil or ruler held at eye-level and measuring the proportions on it with your thumb. If you use a ruler you can actually read off the various proportions.

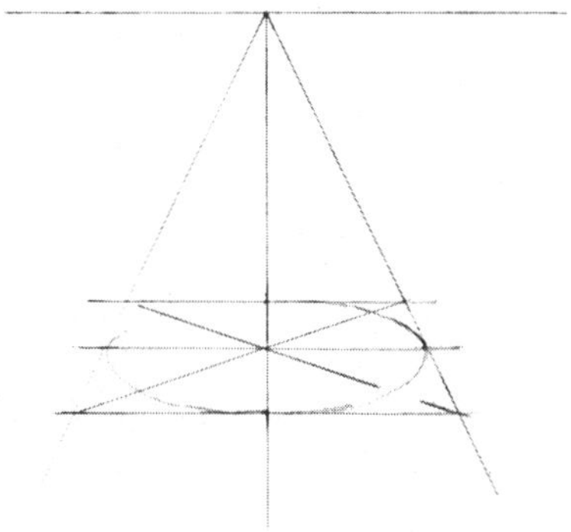

The same applies when, for example, you draw the foreshortened form of a bird. You will tend to draw it the shape you know it to be rather than the shape it appears to be from your viewpoint. Again, measuring one proportion against another will help you to make your drawing look right.

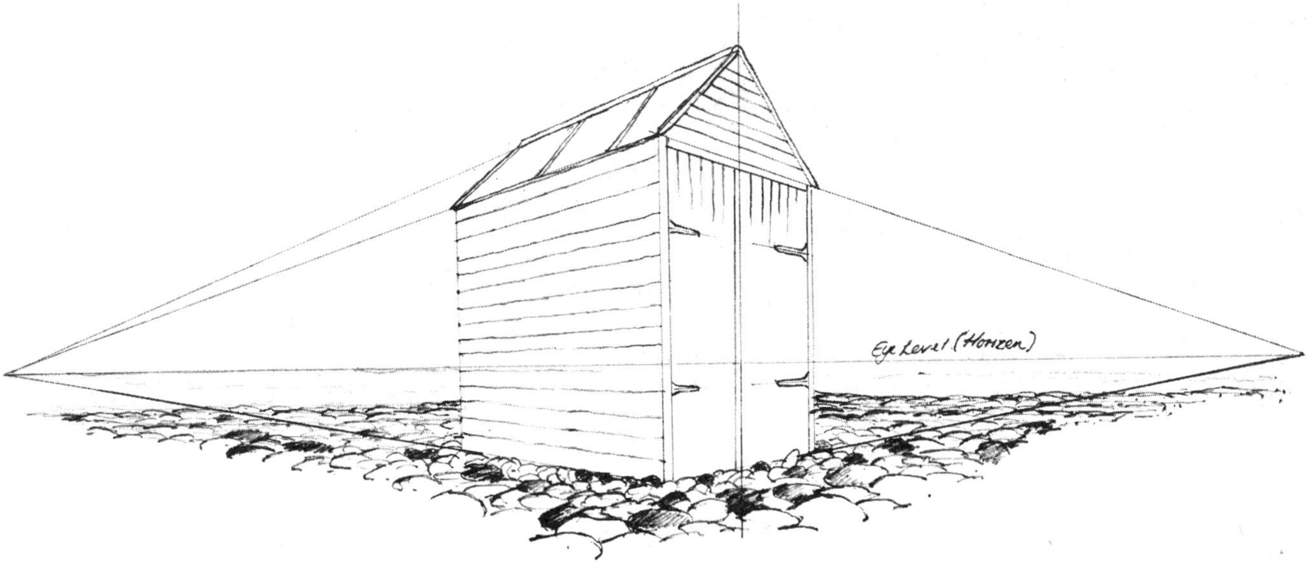

Masses and planes

One point to mention again: all receding parallel lines have the same vanishing point. In this drawing of a breakwater, for instance, this rule applies to all the horizontal edges — including the irregular lines of the cliff-top and of the waves.

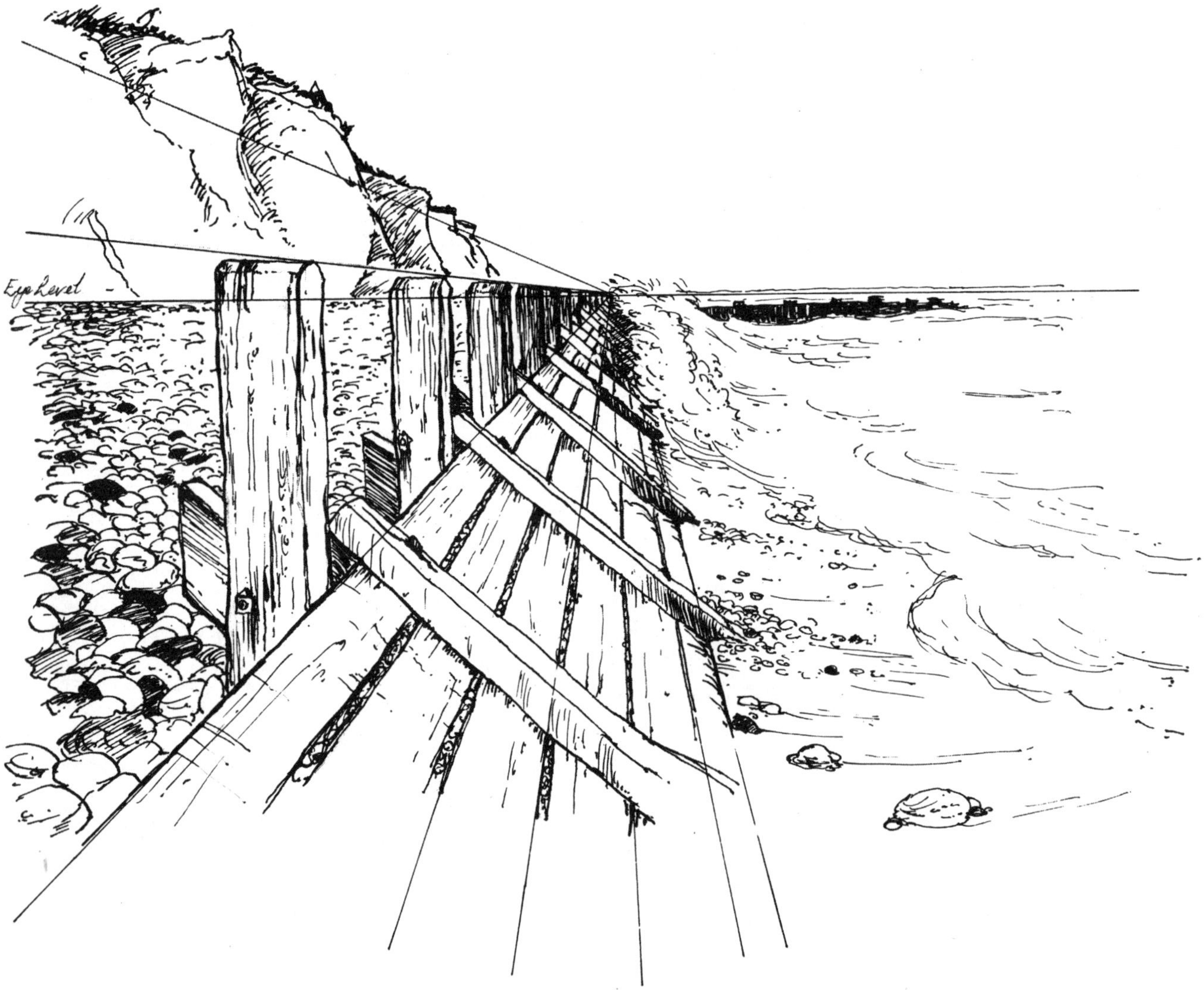

An understanding of the masses and planes of your subject is essential to give your drawing form and conviction. This is clearly seen in the drawing of a cube. But for a more complex form such as a stone, line can be used in the same way to suggest surface and volume. Look carefully for the points at which the surface planes change direction and then let your line describe the form and volume.

When you add tone to a drawing it must convey masses and planes as well as light and shade. Varying the direction of the shading lines helps to indicate irregularities of form.

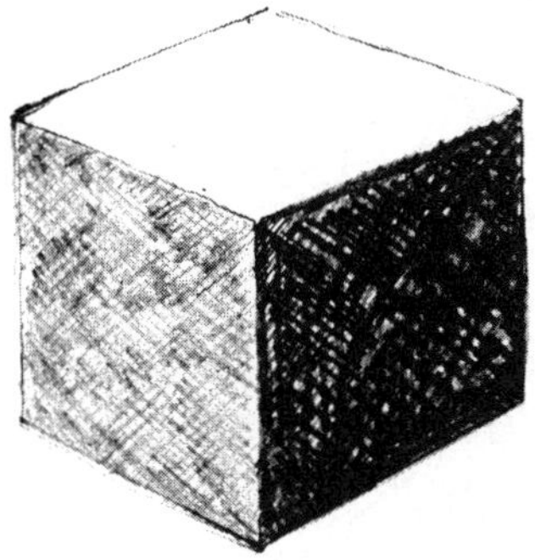

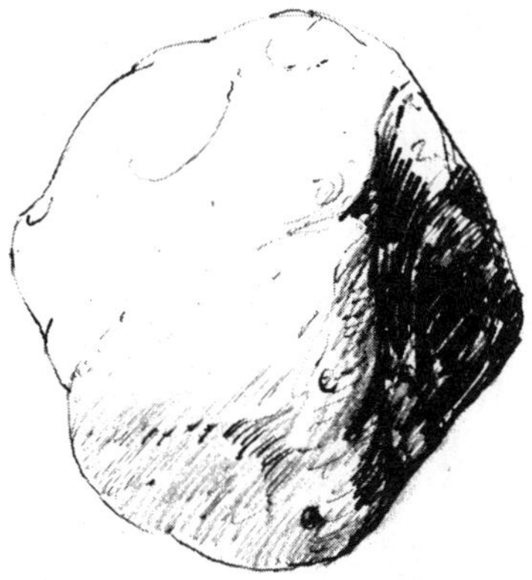

Try drawing stones with different patterns. It is easy to be confused about the difference between colour and light and shade, so try to be aware of this.

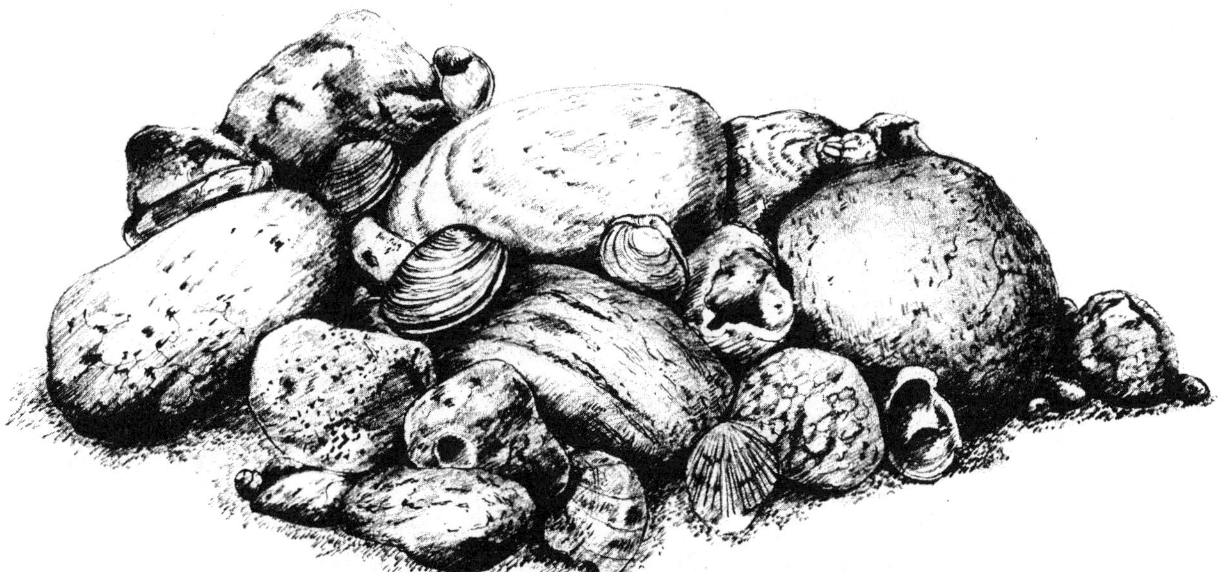

Building up a drawing: 1

Pebbles

Before trying anything as ambitious as a whole pebble beach, draw some single stones. Start with the basic lines and then build up your drawing to give it form and volume and to indicate surface texture. The light is normally very bright by the sea, so use a soft pencil (2B or 3B) to give greater contrast between light and shade.

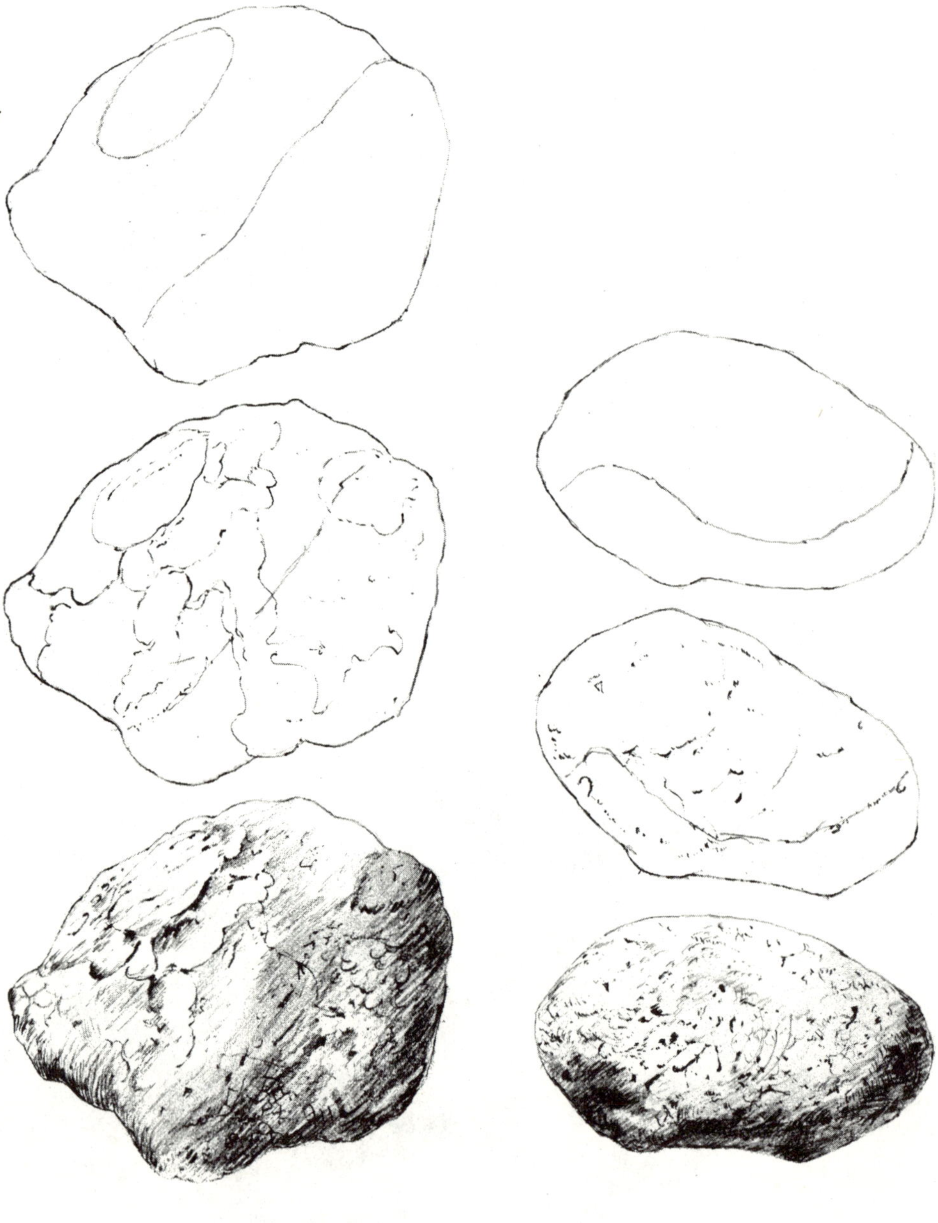

As you gain confidence, try small groups of four or five pebbles. Once again, start with the basic lines; looking through half-closed eyes at your subject will help to shut out most of the detail and show you the essential shapes.

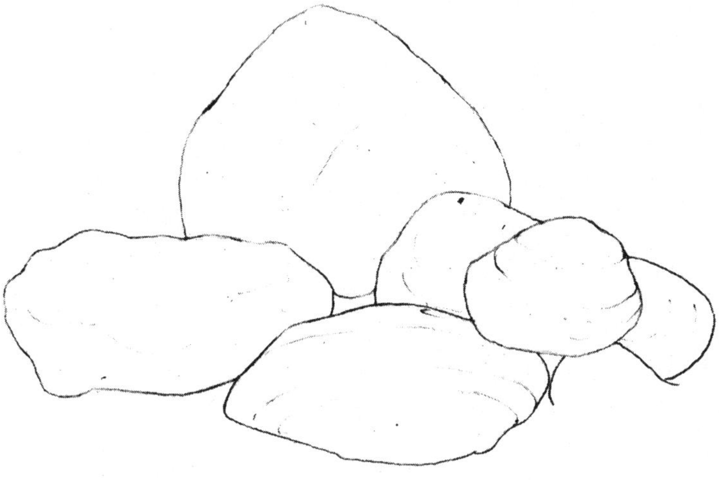

Remember not to make the mistake of confusing colour with light and shade. Here just the main areas of shadow have been put in.

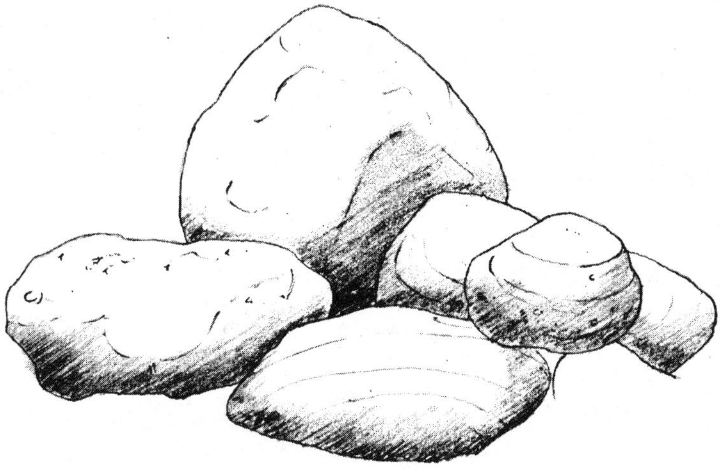

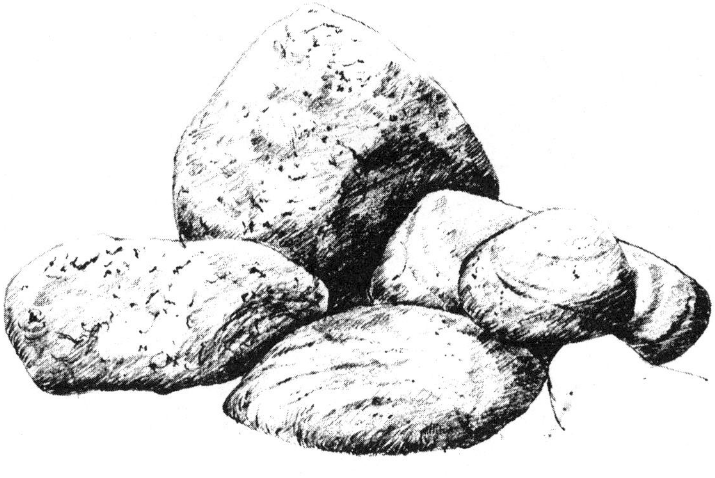

Building up a drawing: 2

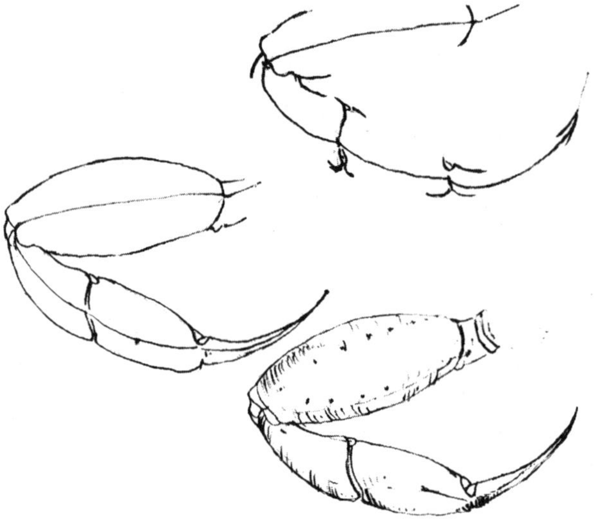

Crabs

Dead crabs are easily found on the shore and are an excellent subject for exploration and detailed drawing. Don't be put off by their apparently complex structure; they are for the most part symmetrical. And don't be afraid to put in imaginary lines to help you establish the form.

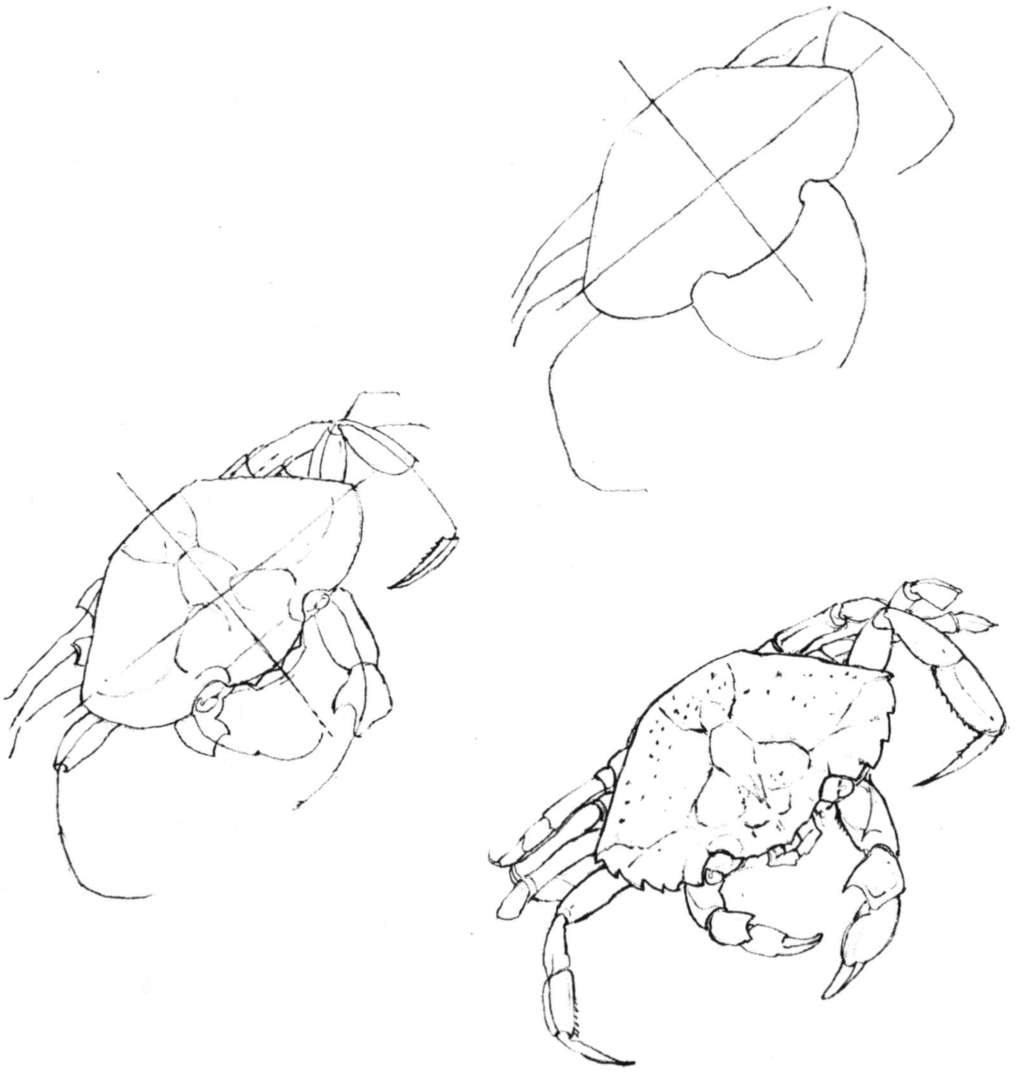

Even though a crab has eight legs, once you have worked out the structure of one the others should present few problems. Examine the claws and joints closely so that you understand how they work.

Try drawing the crab from different view points. For this kind of detailed drawing of a complex subject you need a fine line — a sharp pencil or a fine pen is ideal.

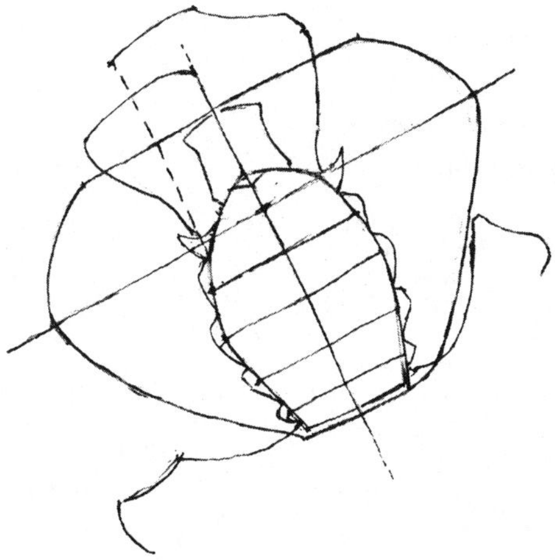

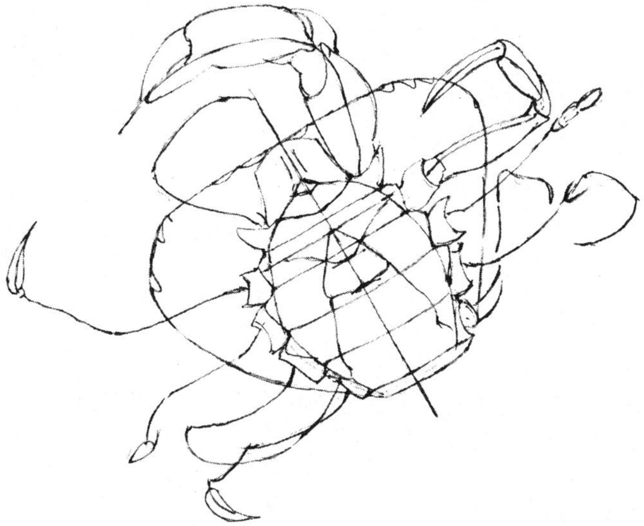

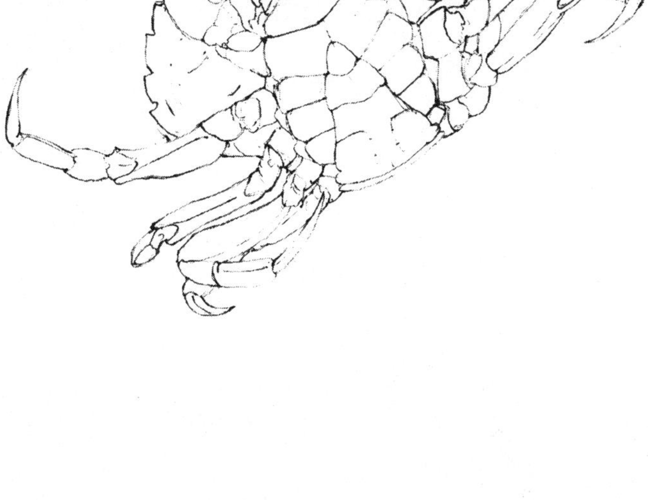

Building up a drawing: 3

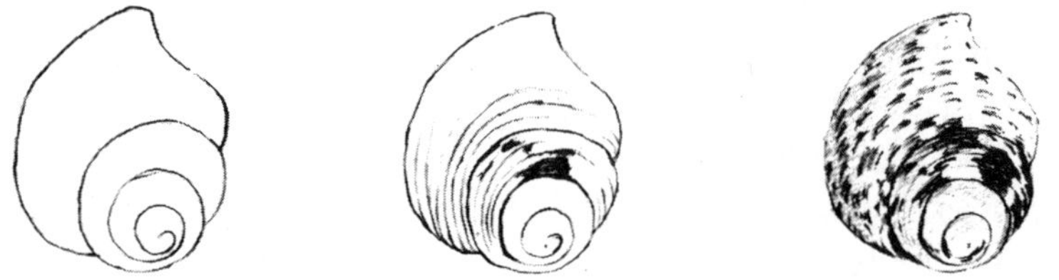

Shells
Shells are fascinating to draw, with their delicate structure and beautiful markings. As with the pebbles, try drawing individual shells before attempting a group.

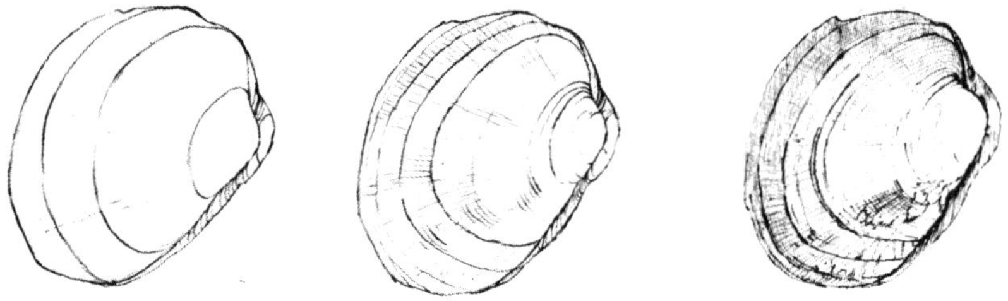

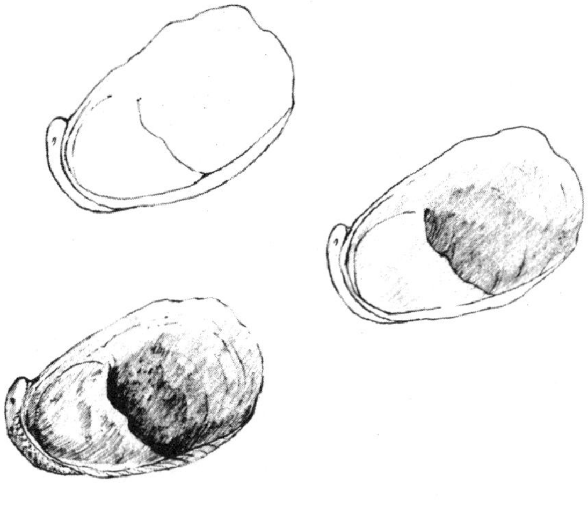

The slipper limpet (right), which can often be found in large numbers on the beach, is a good shell to start off with. Having established the basic shape, use the pattern on the shell to describe its form.

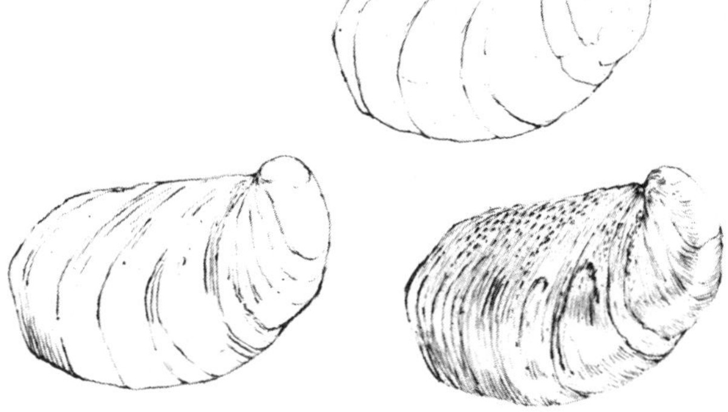

With spiral shells such as the periwinkle and whelk, it helps to remember the spiral structure when looking at the exterior shape. Again, notice how the pattern describes the form. (More examples of shell structure are shown on pages 20 and 21.)

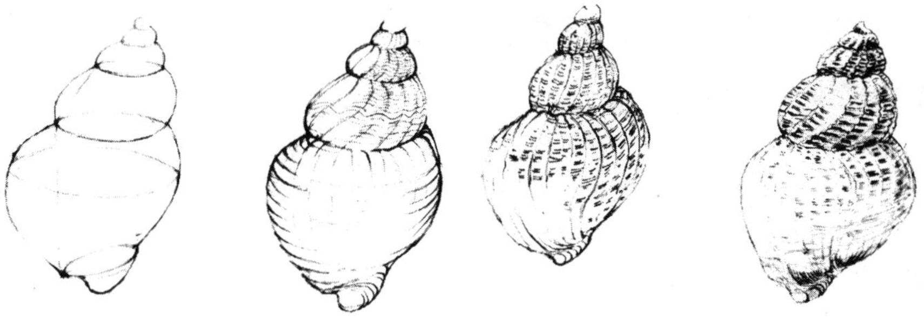

Try drawing a group of pebbles, shells and perhaps a dead crab. As you become more experienced in drawing a variety of subjects you can experiment with more ambitious compositions.

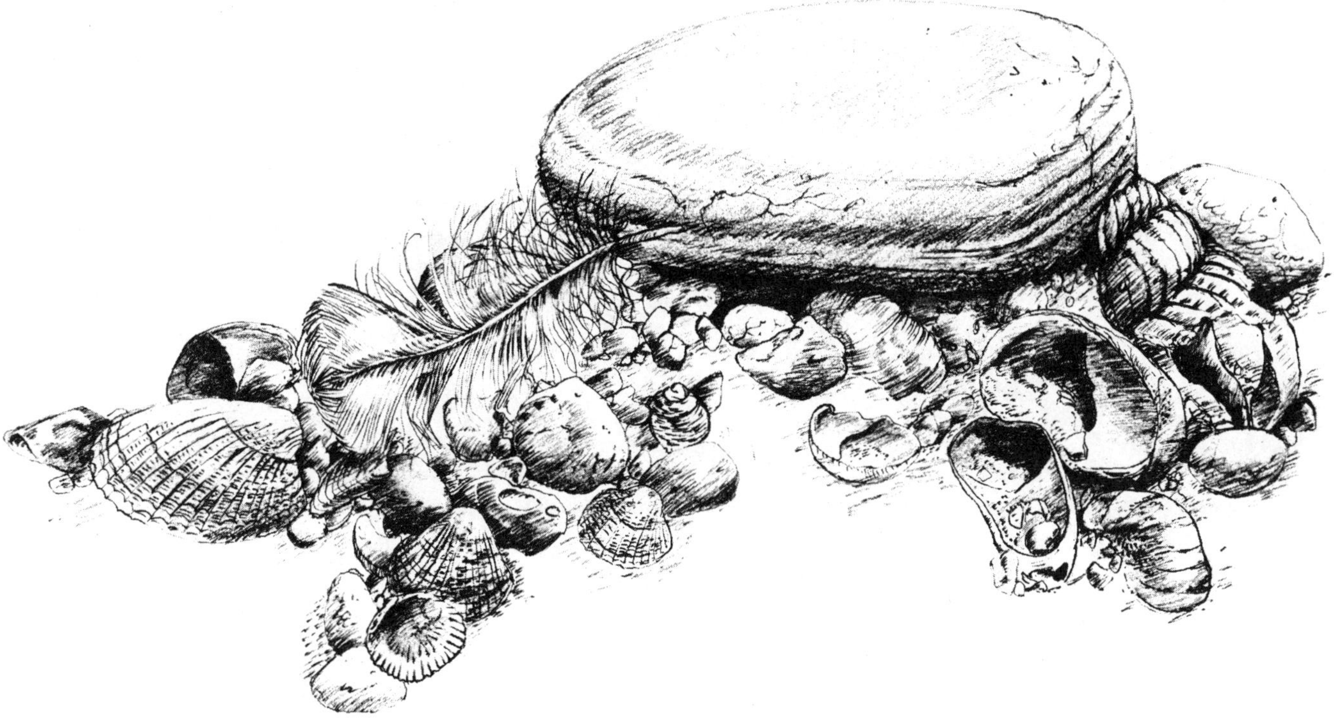

Structure and pattern

Shells

Look closely at the structure of these spiral shells. Broken whelk shells are easy to find and show clearly the wonderfully delicate yet strong internal spiral (below, left).

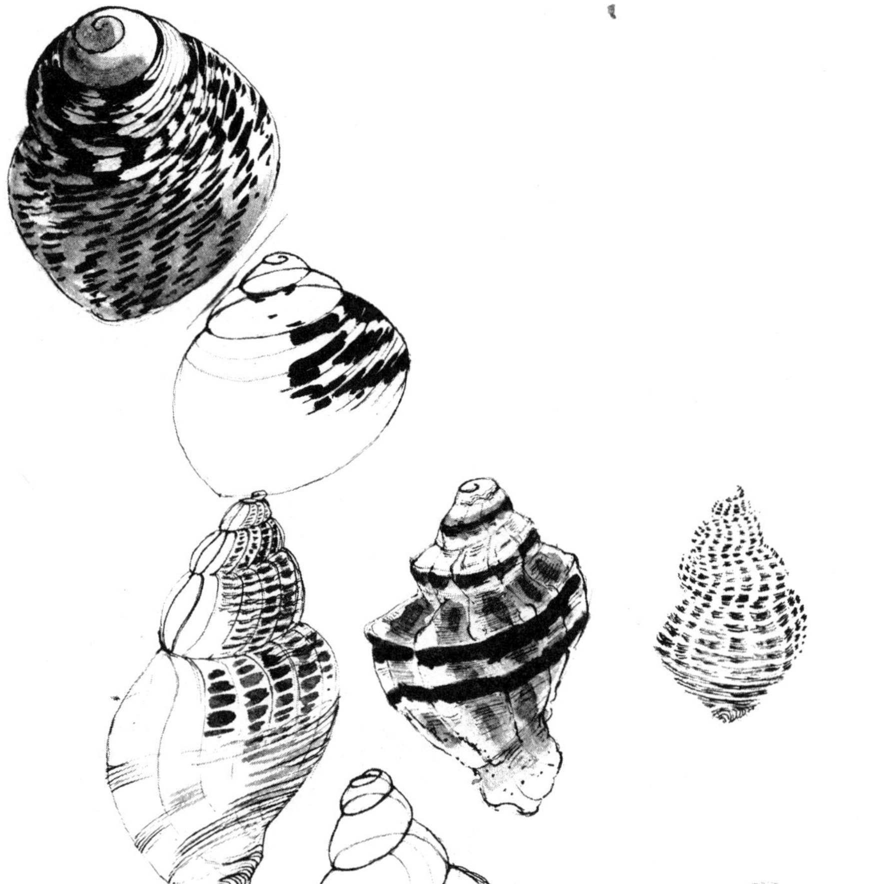

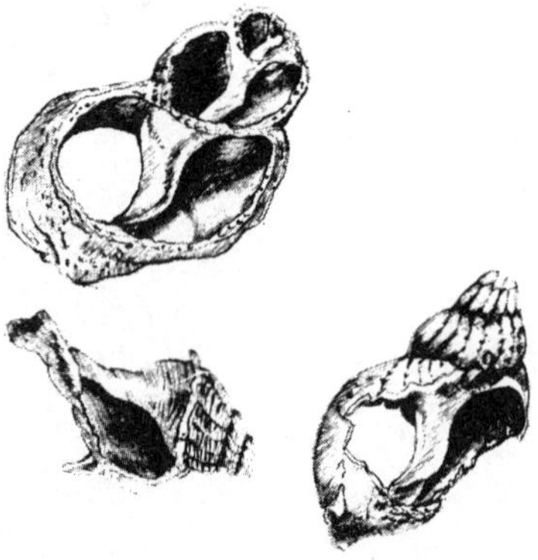

Again, look at the exterior pattern on different shells. Try drawing the shell by its pattern only.

The common piddock and the mussel are bi-valve molluscs whose shells consist of two halves hinged at one point. It is not necessary to put in every ridge of the shell; to hint at the pattern with a few careful lines is much more convincing.

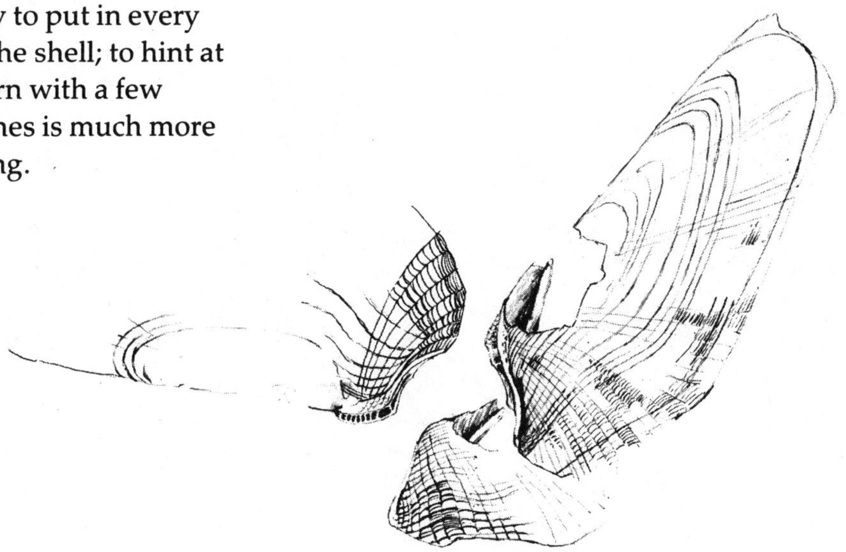

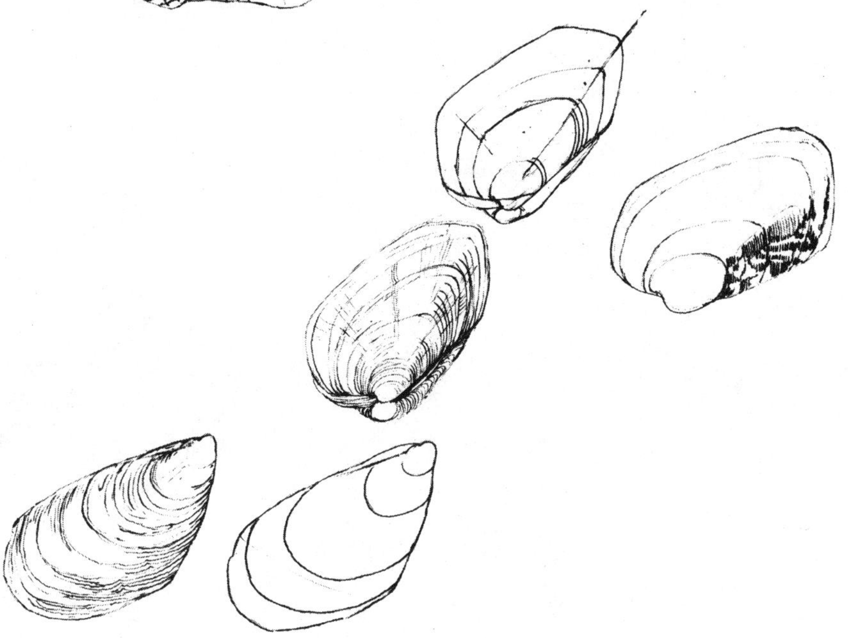

Sand and shingle

As the tide goes out over a sandy beach the constant lapping of the receding waves leaves rippling patterns in the sand. Similar patterns are made by the wind whipping over dry sand dunes. A flat expanse of sand, made up of so many minute particles, is difficult to draw, but these ripples provide interesting forms.

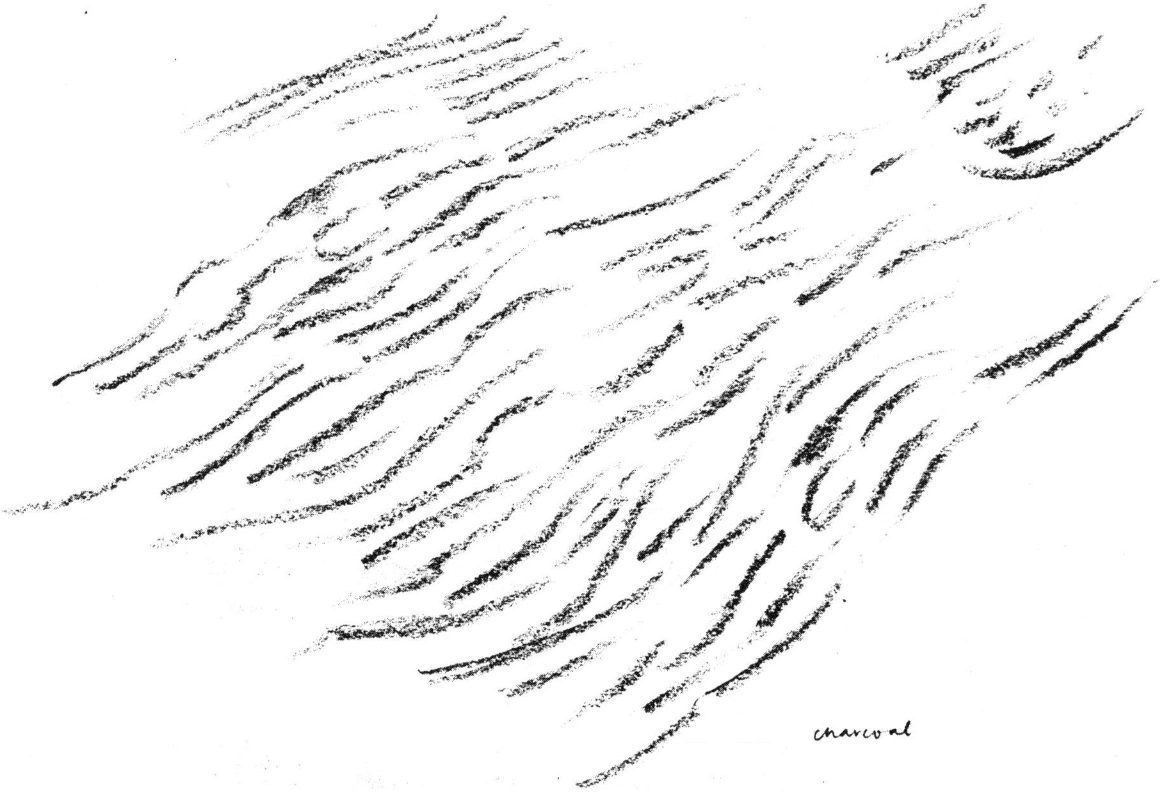

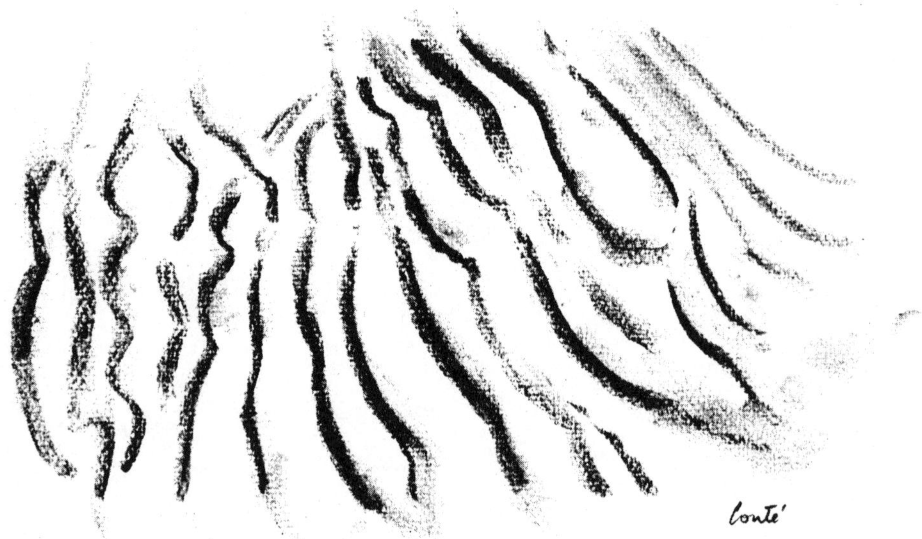

Charcoal or Conté are both good for drawing sand ripples. You can use the side of the charcoal or crayon as well as the tip. It is easy to lose your place when drawing a large patterned area, so choose a prominent or unusual ridge that stands out from the rest as a starting point to which you can relate the rest of your drawing.

Notice how, on wet sand, the tops of the ridges reflect the light and there is greater contrast between light and dark areas.

Drawing a large area of shingle may seem a daunting task at first. It is clearly impossible to draw every pebble, so draw only what you see from an overall viewpoint, and forget about detail. Remember that the further away the stones are, the smaller they will appear. Compare the look of the pebbles closest to you with those about fifteen feet away and those in the distance, and remember that they overlap so that only the upper part is visible.

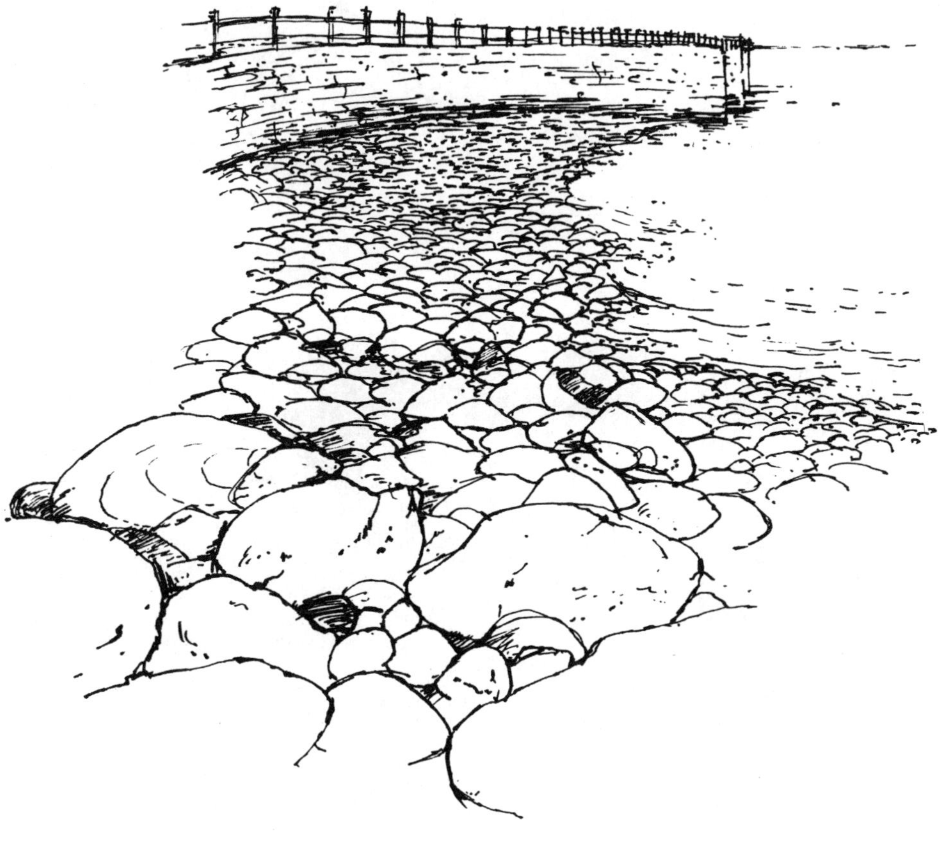

Quick sketches on the spot

The seashore is a good place to draw birds. Unlike shells and stones, sea birds will not stay in one place while you draw them. Watch them carefully as they move and make a series of quick sketches, trying to catch characteristic shapes and positions.

I find an ordinary fountain pen is excellent for quick sketches of this kind. The ink runs freely and does not dry up if you pause to watch your subject. (While you are sharpening your pencil you may miss a wing being stretched or a fish being swallowed.)

From these quick, on-the spot sketches of shags I was able to make up a composition at leisure, using a Gillott 303 and wash.

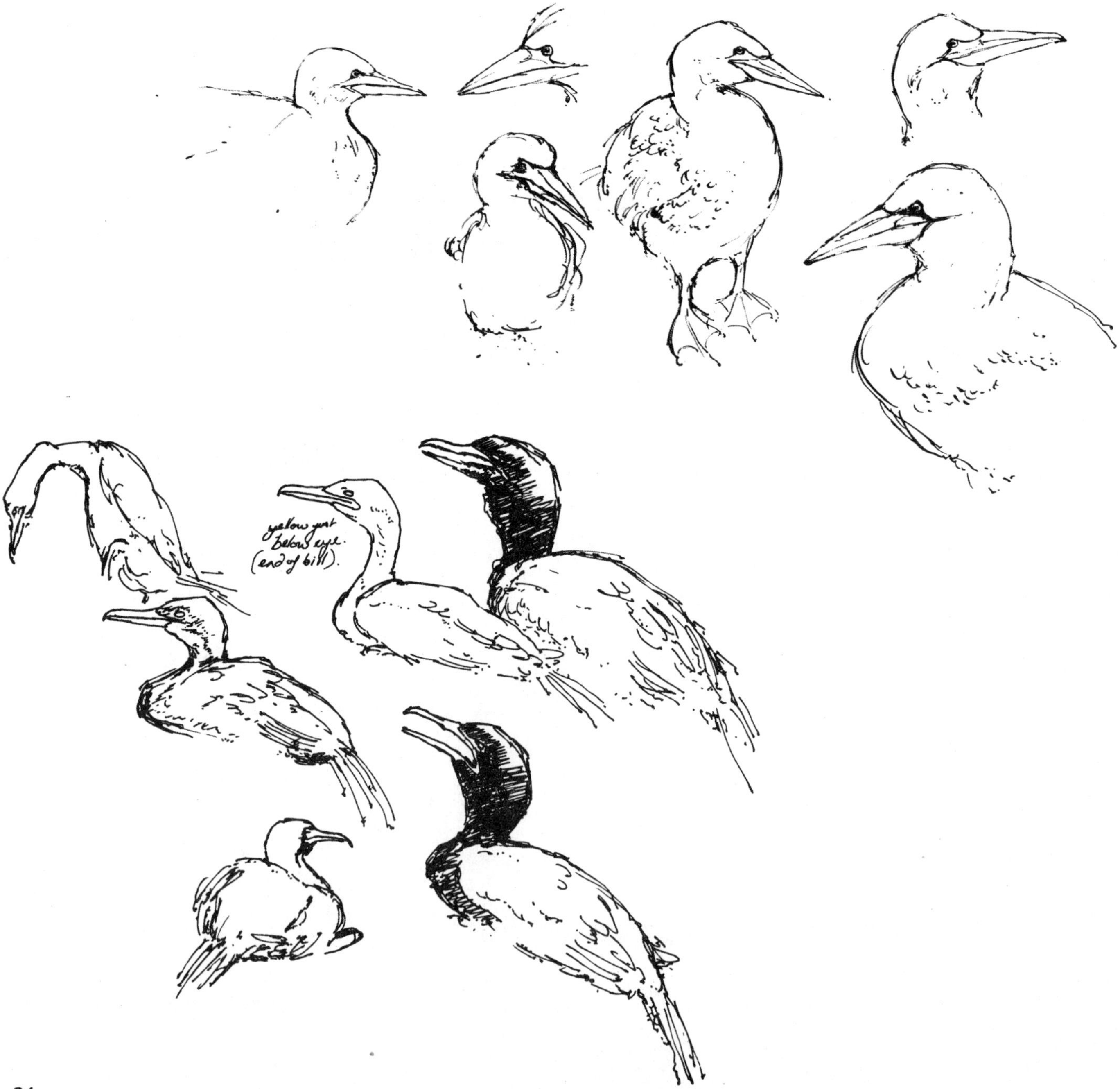

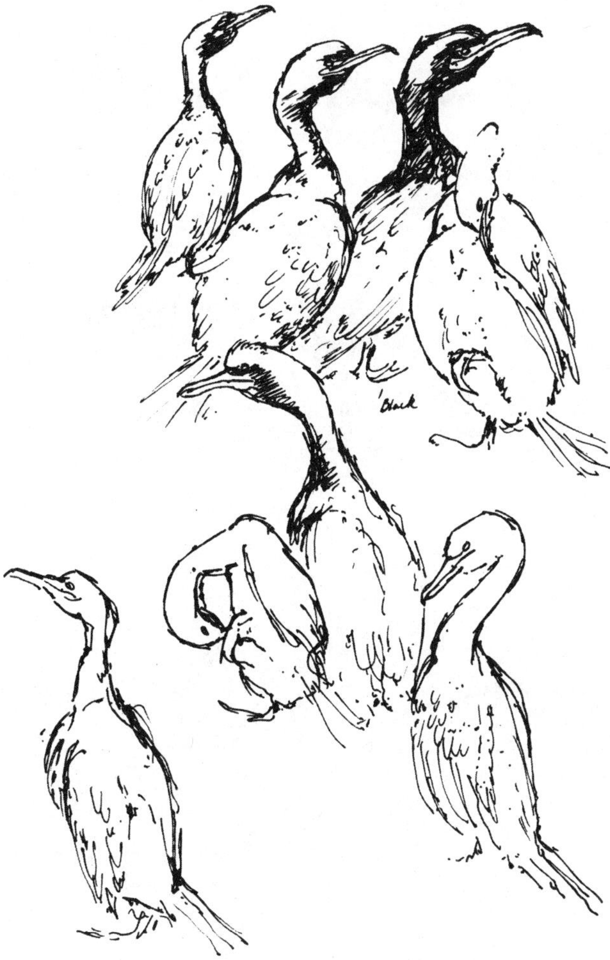
Black

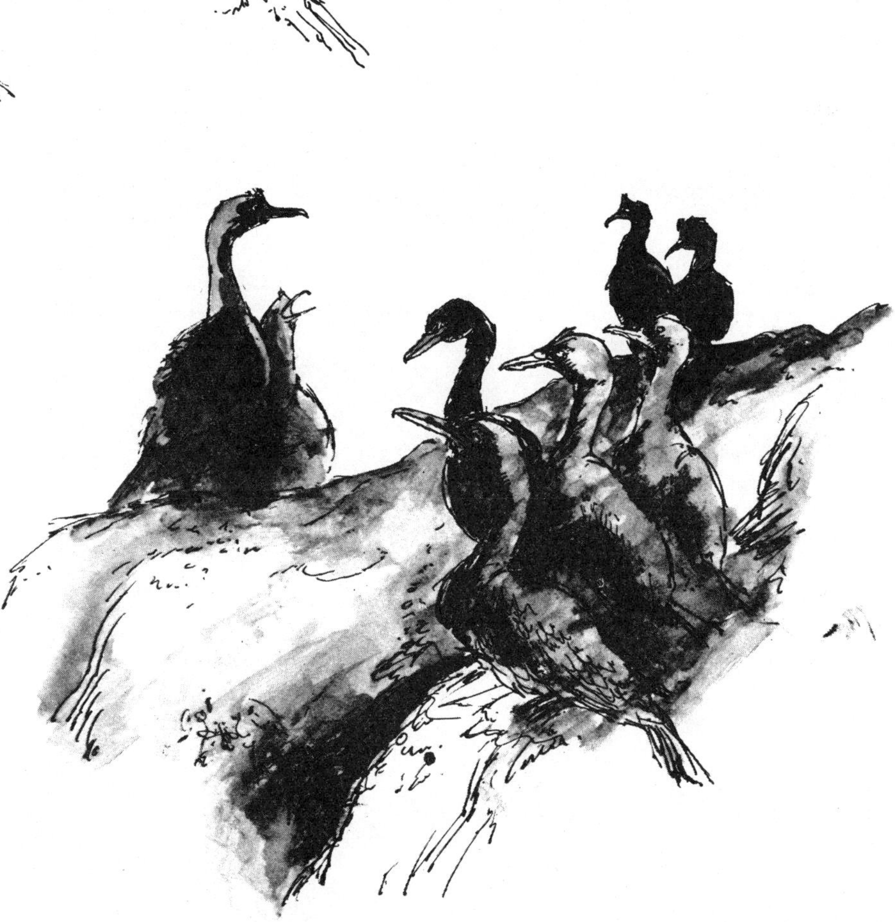

These rough sketches of lapwings and waders, again done with a fountain pen, provide a page of valuable reference showing the birds' characteristic positions. When using these sketches for a finished drawing, it may be necessary to use photographic reference as well for the finer details.

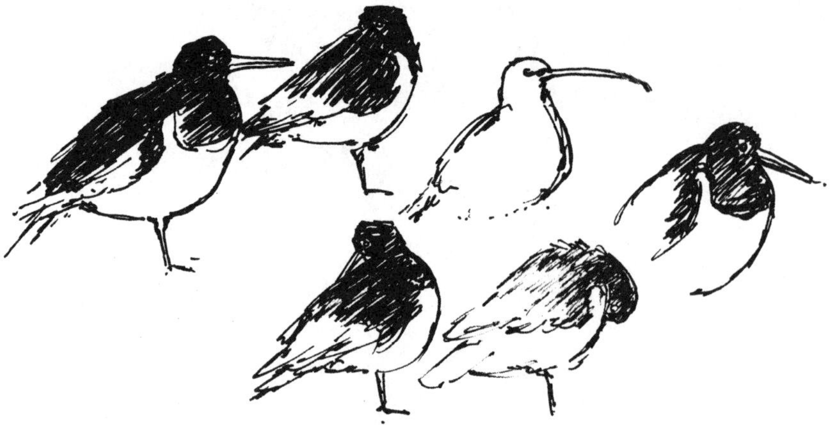

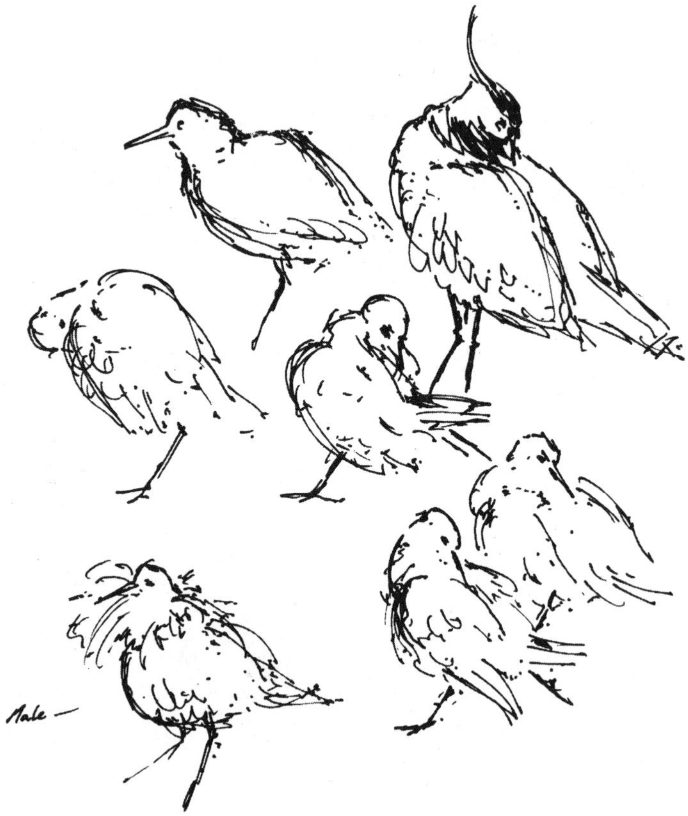

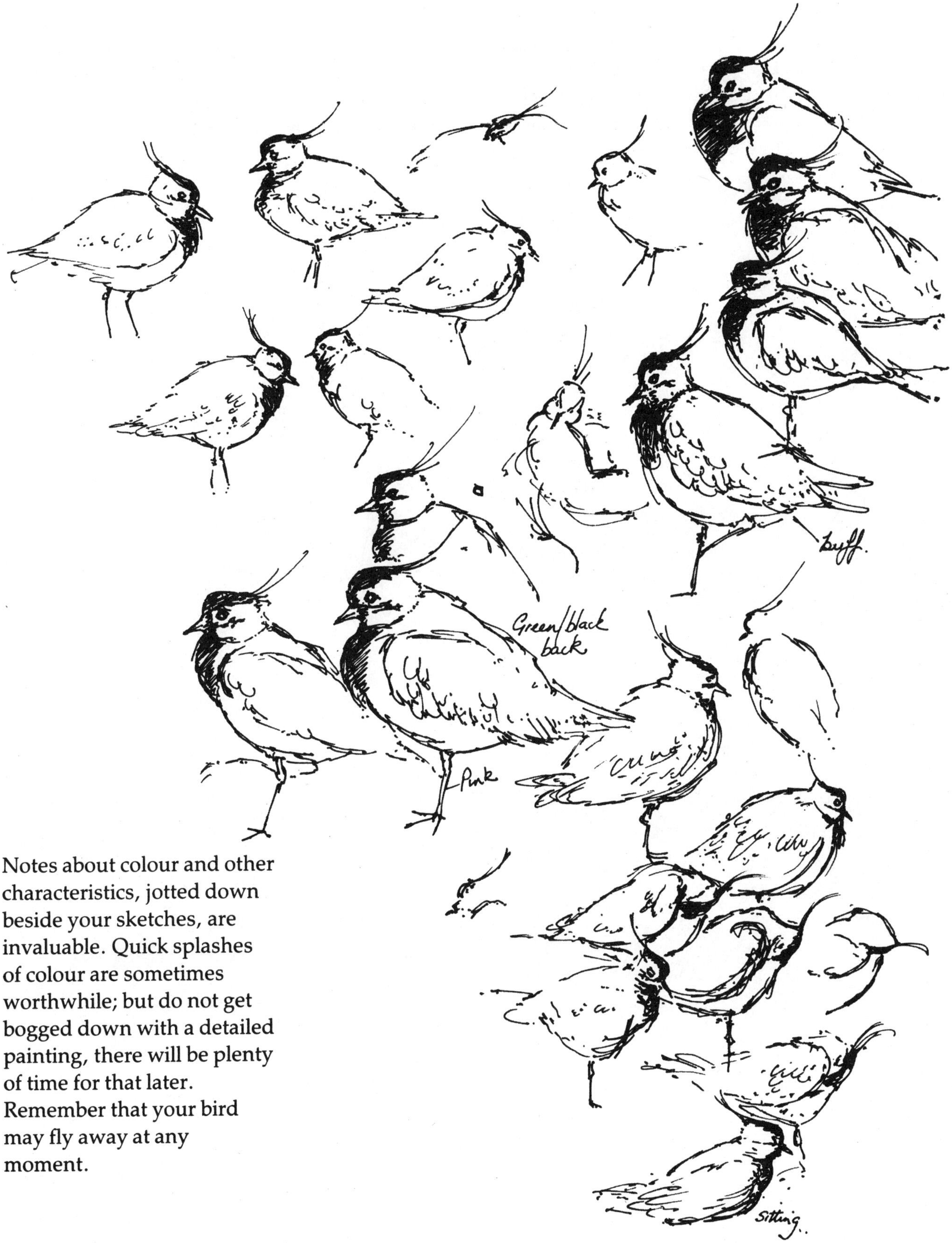

Notes about colour and other characteristics, jotted down beside your sketches, are invaluable. Quick splashes of colour are sometimes worthwhile; but do not get bogged down with a detailed painting, there will be plenty of time for that later. Remember that your bird may fly away at any moment.

Many beaches have sand dunes and most sand dunes have rabbits. Rabbits are great fun to draw, but often you have time to do little more than a scribble before your subject disappears behind a tuft of grass. Don't get discouraged — start as many different sketches on the same page as you need. You may be able to go back to any one of them when the rabbit resumes that position.

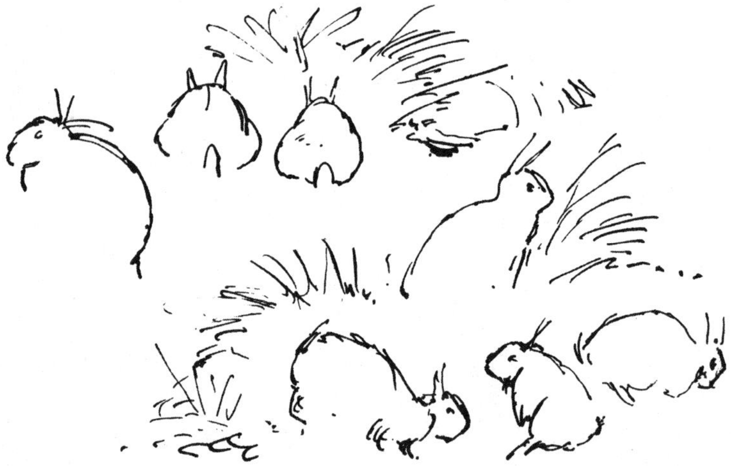

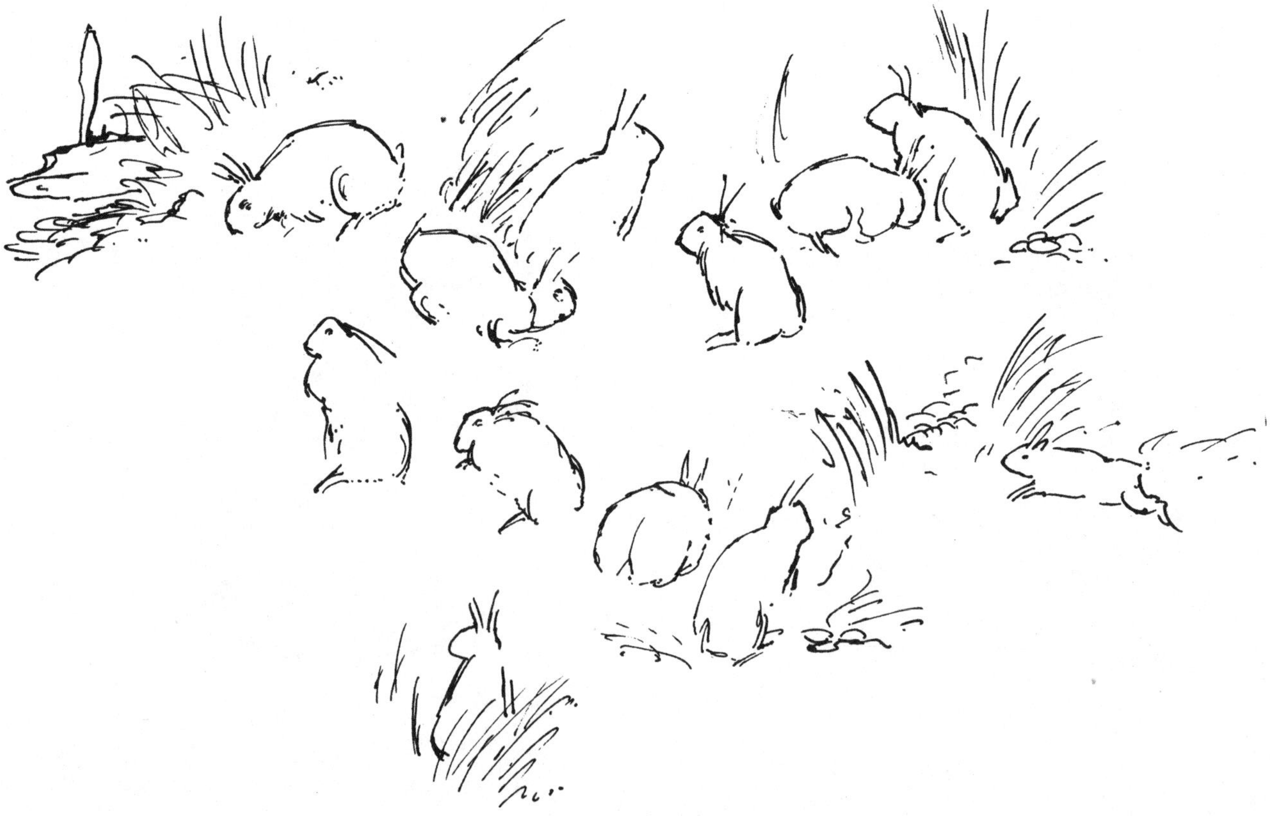

By looking and drawing quickly in this way you will become really familiar with your subject. Your ability to catch essential features will develop rapidly and your confidence will increase.

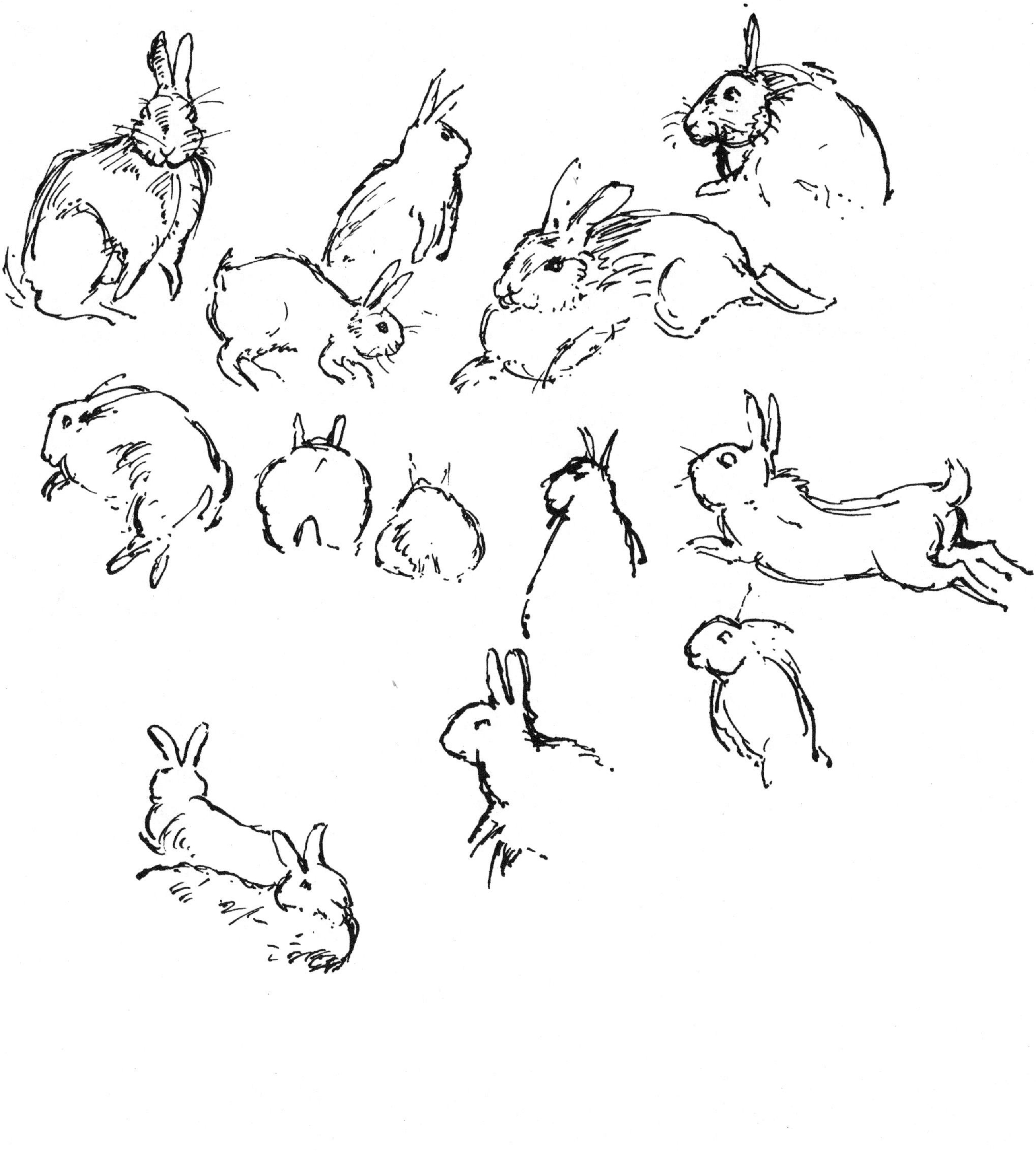

More careful drawing

Fish

Fish can often be found on the seashore — but if you want to draw them complete with eyes you must find them before the squabbling gulls get at them.

A Gillott 303 was used for these drawings of a plaice, a flat fish which starts life with an eye on each side of its head. As it grows it takes to lying on its side on the bottom of the sea, and one eye twists round to produce that peculiar crooked gaze.

Look carefully at the pattern of the scales. They are irregular and tend to be much smaller around the fins and tail.

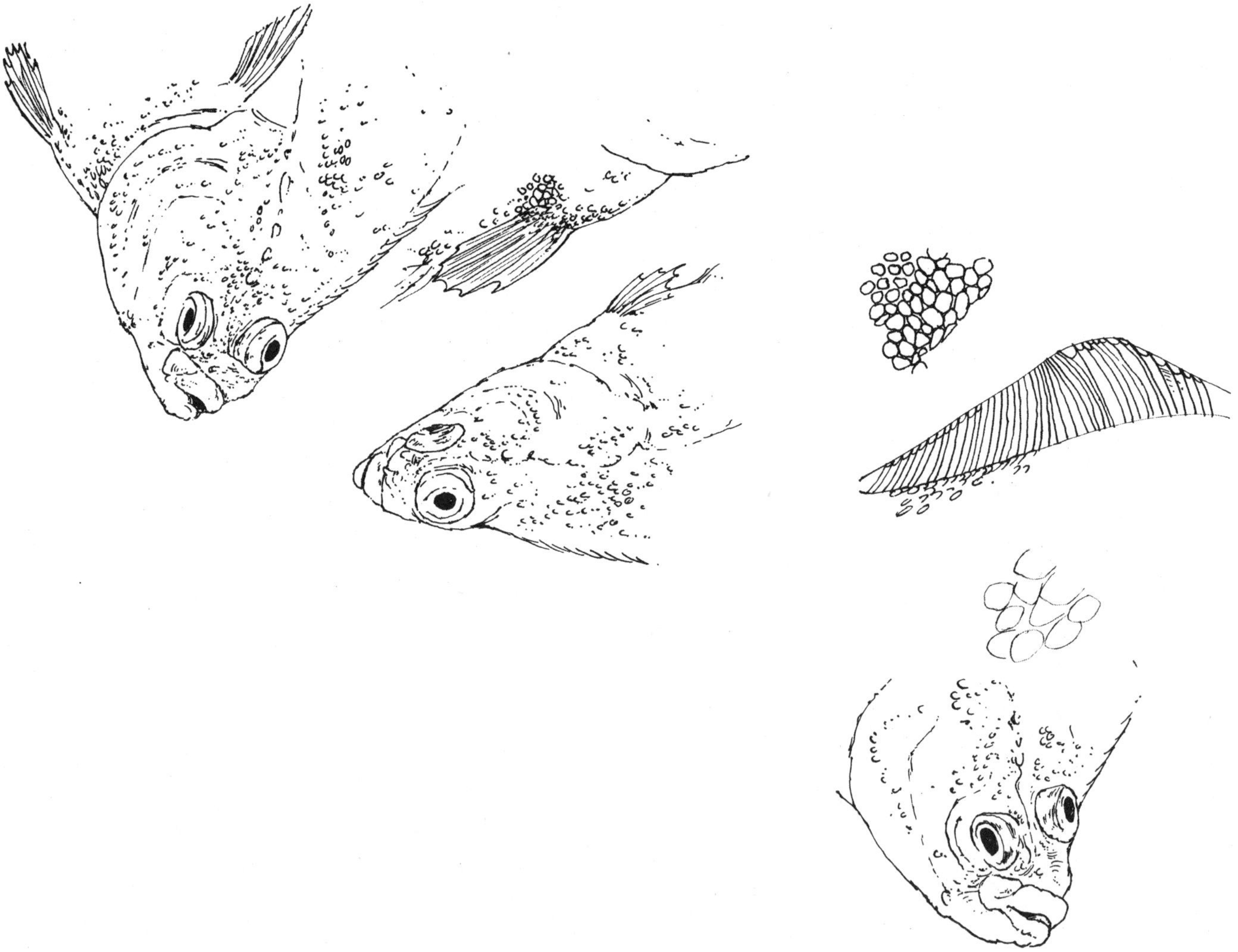

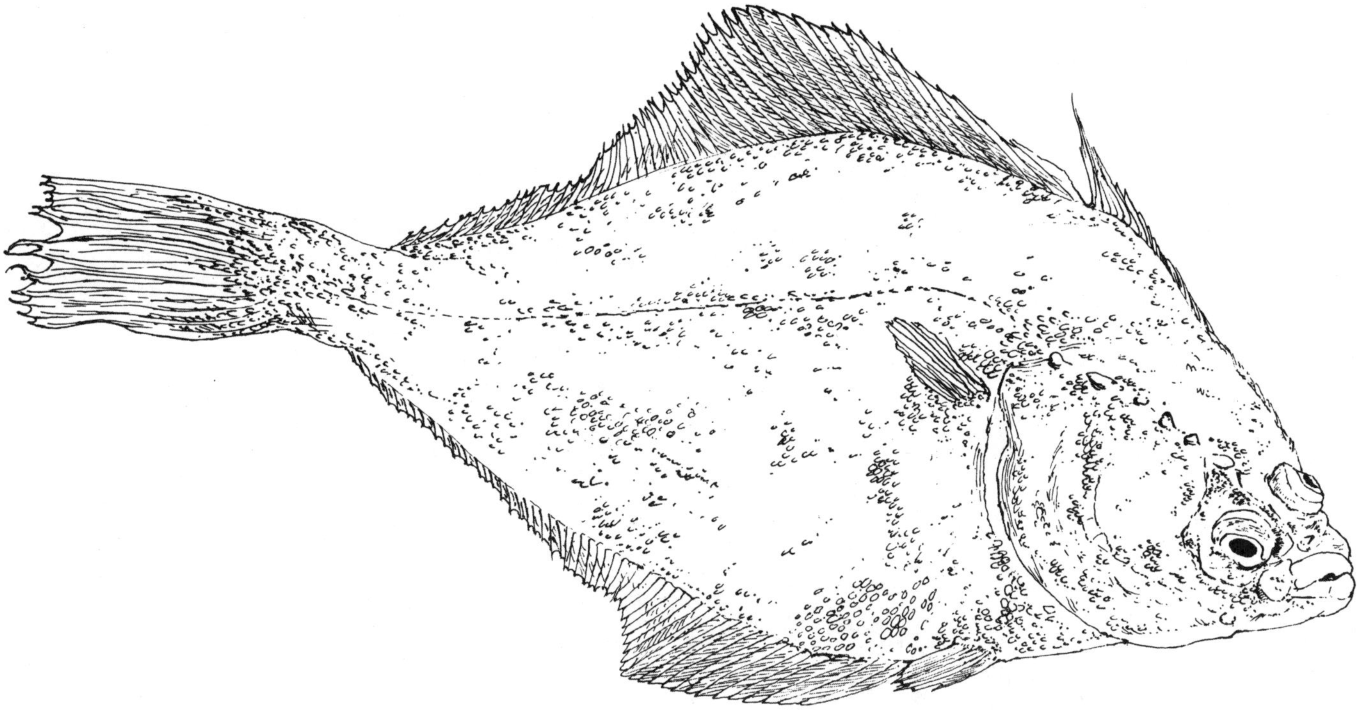

The mackerel is a good example of a normal-looking fish. With it's beautifully patterned back, it makes an interesting subject to draw.

Here I've used a B pencil; it gives an adequate range of tone but can also be used for details such as the fins and tail without becoming messy and smudged.

Draw the mackerel from several viewpoints. Look at the structure of head and tail. Notice the curve of the body and use shading to indicate the roundness of the form.

You could keep a sketchbook in which to build up a collection of different types of fish. To learn more about the shape and movement of live fish, go to an aquarium and watch them swimming about.

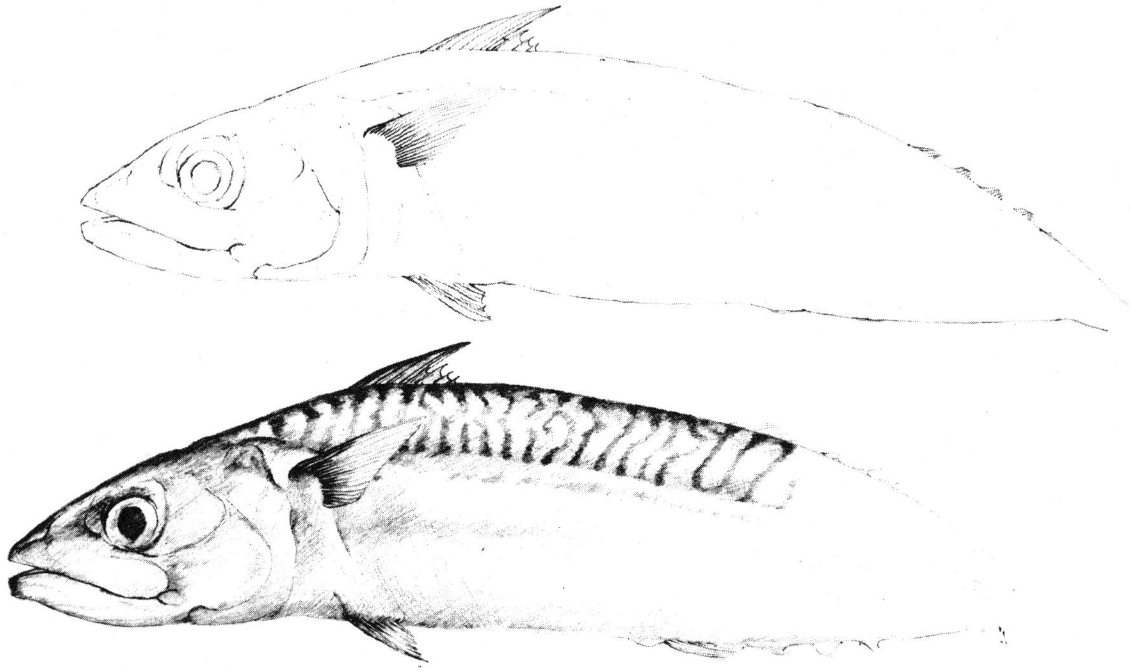

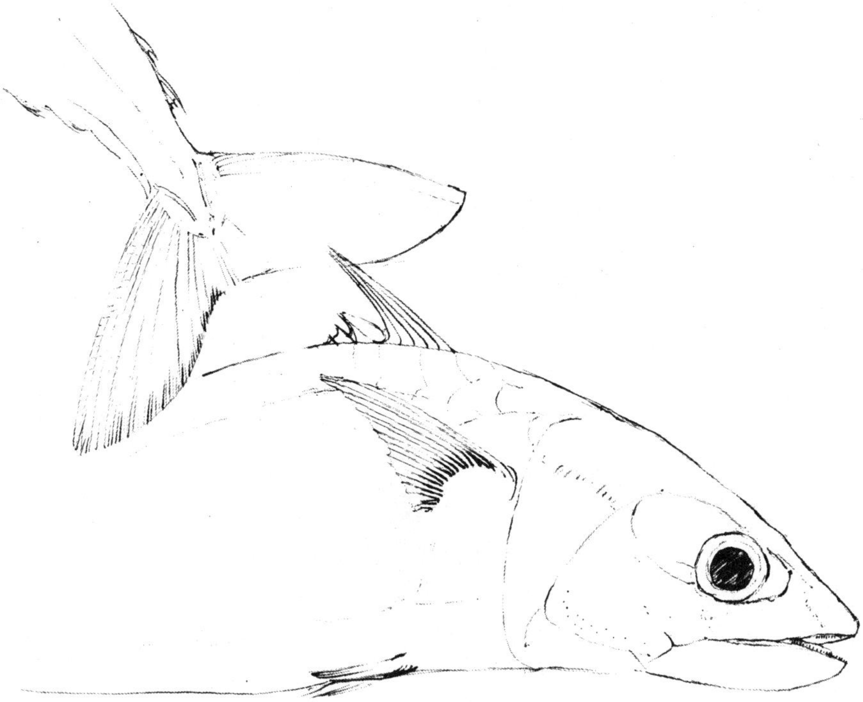

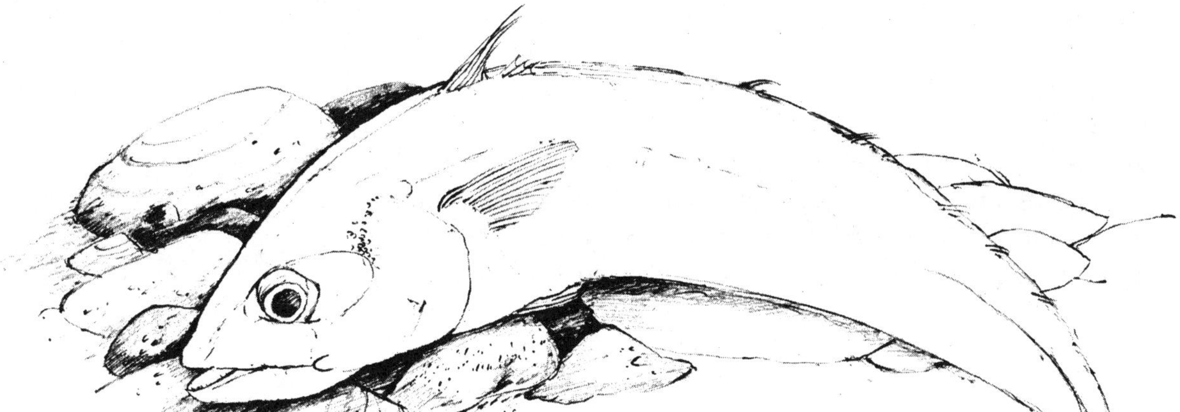

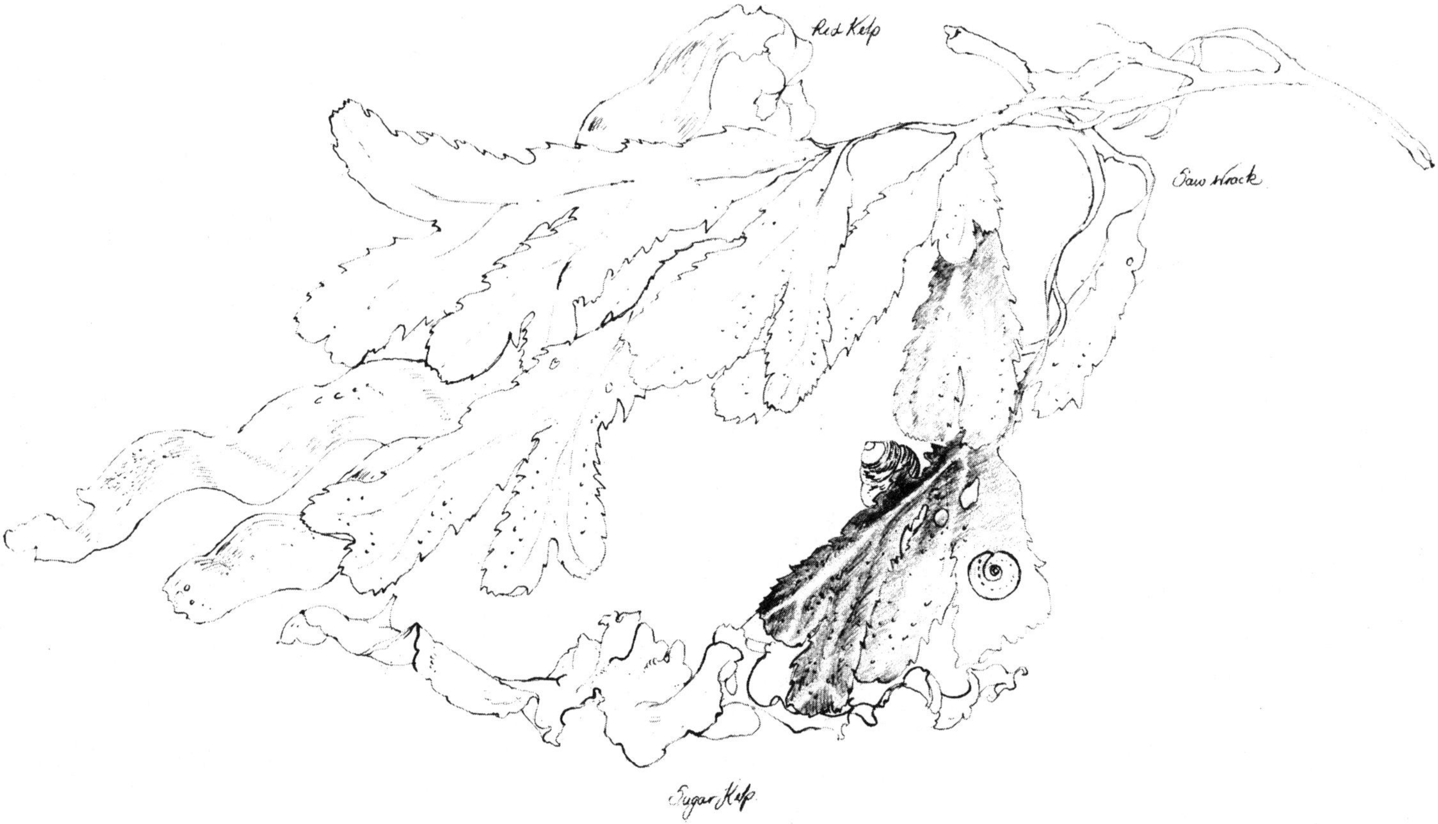

Seaweed

At low tide, seaweed can often be found in large masses along the shore, in pools and on the rocks. 'Seaweed' is a collective term for many different kinds of plants. Draw as many different types as you can find. These four varieties were all found on the same beach.

The frilly, twisting shapes of sugar kelp are easily recognisable.

Bladder wrack (opposite) is good to draw, with its bubbly leaves. It is quite a complicated plant, so take it step by step — do not try to draw the whole mass straight away. Start with an easily identifiable piece and relate the rest of your drawing to this as you work. When you have drawn the main shapes, tone and texture can be added.

Sea birds can often be seen hunting for the periwinkles and crabs that feed or hide in tangled clumps of seaweed.

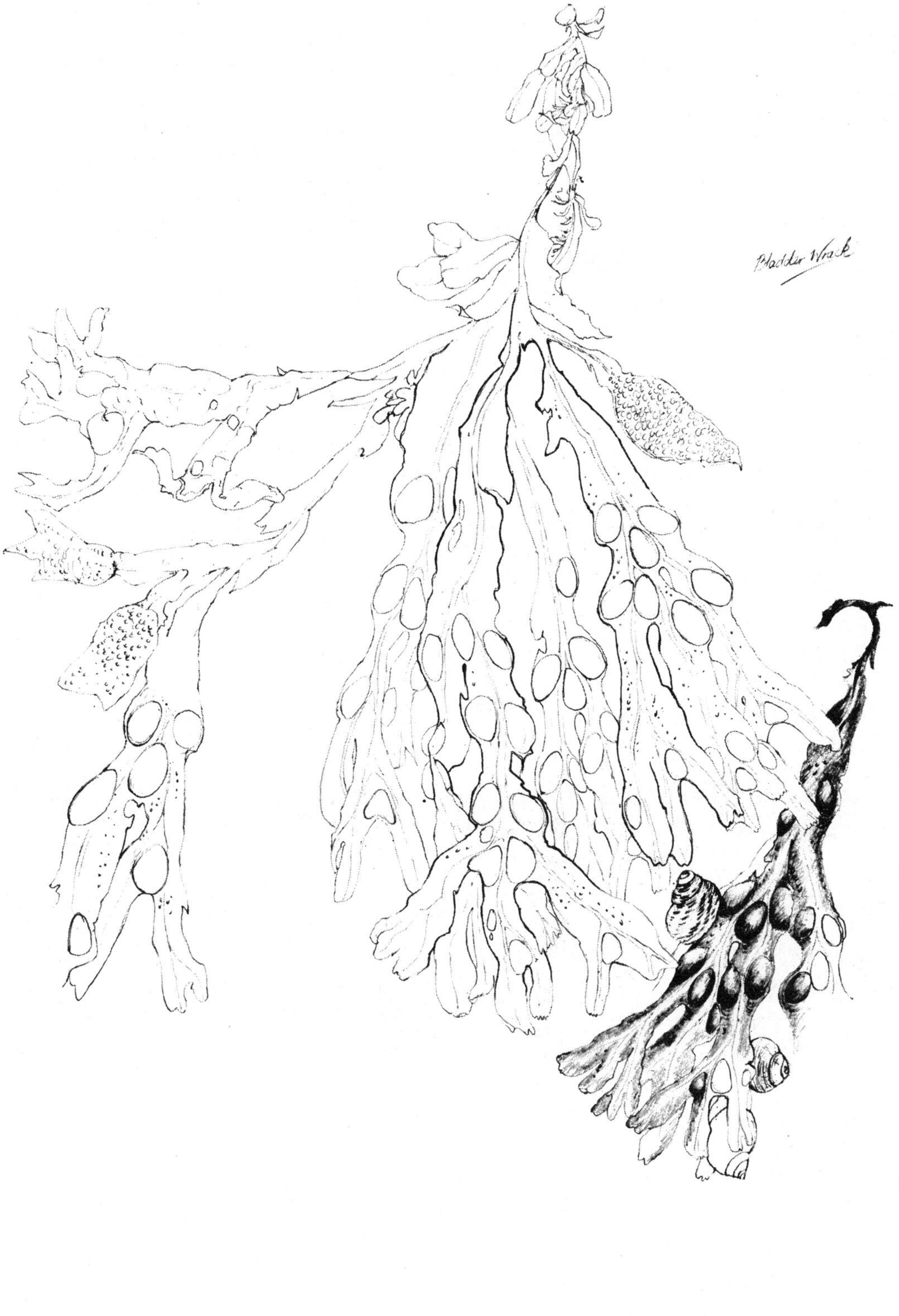
Bladder Wrack

Same subject, different media

Make a habit of experimenting with different media rather than always drawing in pencil. This will extend the range of your ability and you may find that trying something new will produce unexpected results.

For the combination of soft sand and spiky grass in sand dunes I have tried three possibilities. A Gillott 303 pen, or a sharp pencil, seemed ideal for drawing the grass blown by a determined sea breeze.

The texture of sand rippled into patterns can be sketched quickly with a Conté stick (see page 22), using a sharp Conté pencil for the grass.

Try combining different media in the same drawing for varied effects and textures.

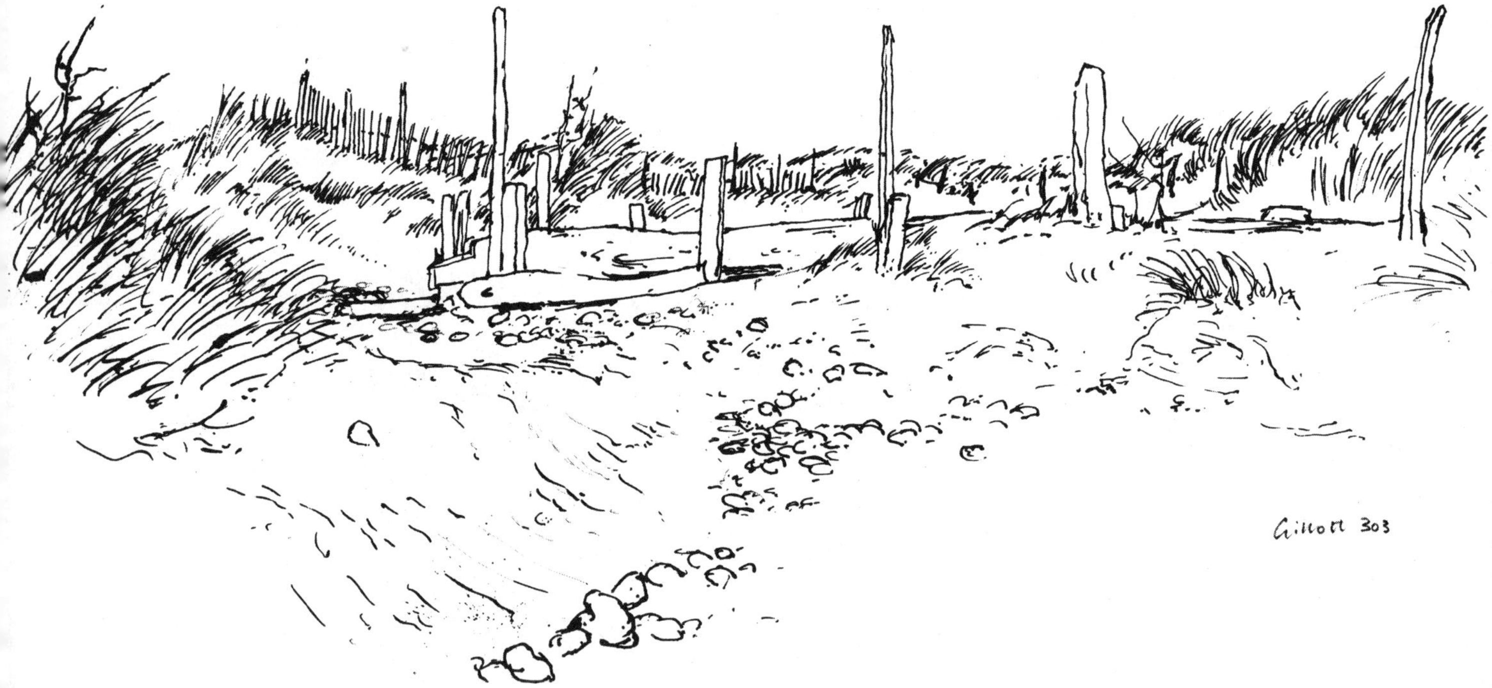

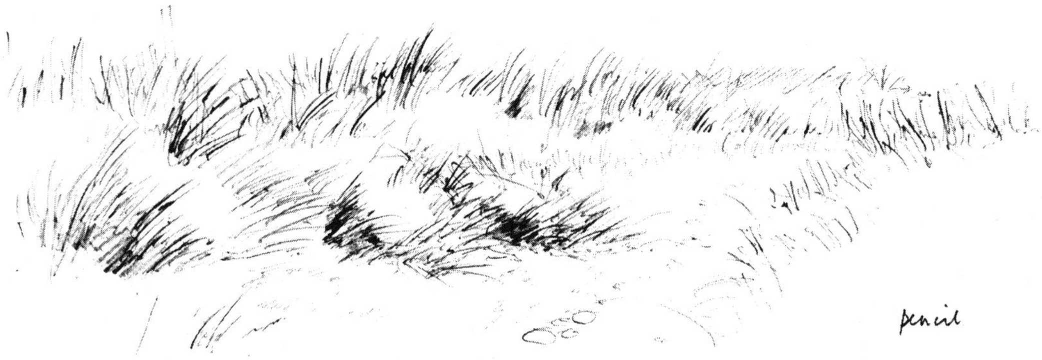
pencil

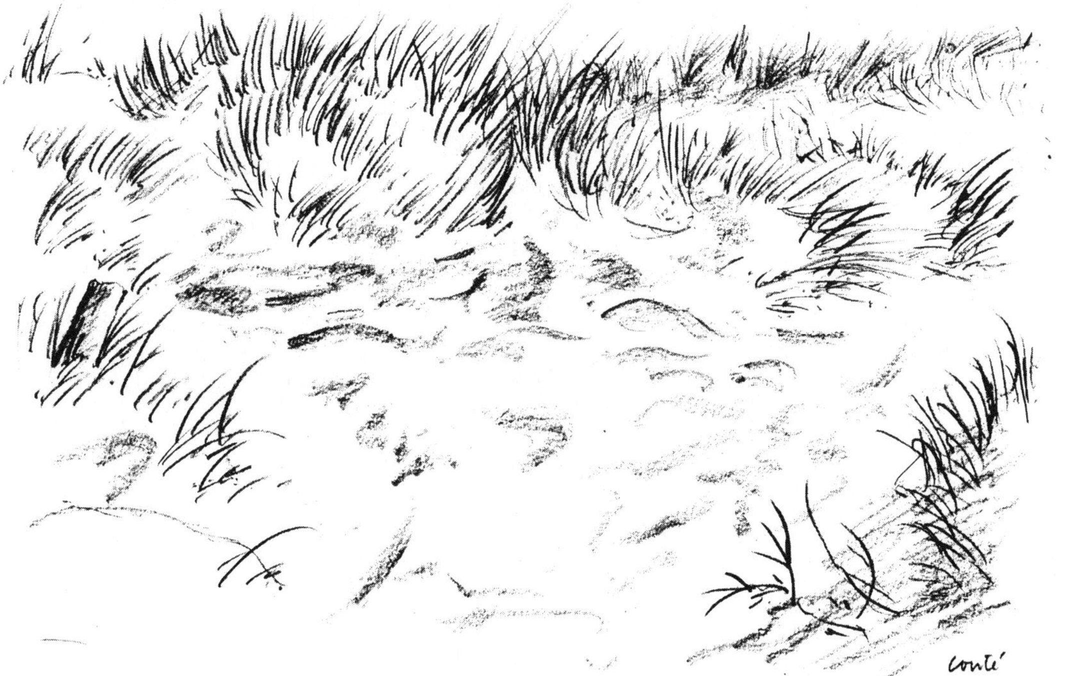
conté

Collecting

It is not always possible to draw on the beach — maybe you haven't enough time, the tide is coming in, or the weather is bad. But many objects besides stone and shells can be collected and taken home to be studied and drawn in detail.

The egg sacs of the dog fish, sometimes known as 'mermaids' purses', are interesting shapes with curly tendrils. Try adding wash to a pen and ink drawing to add tone and texture.

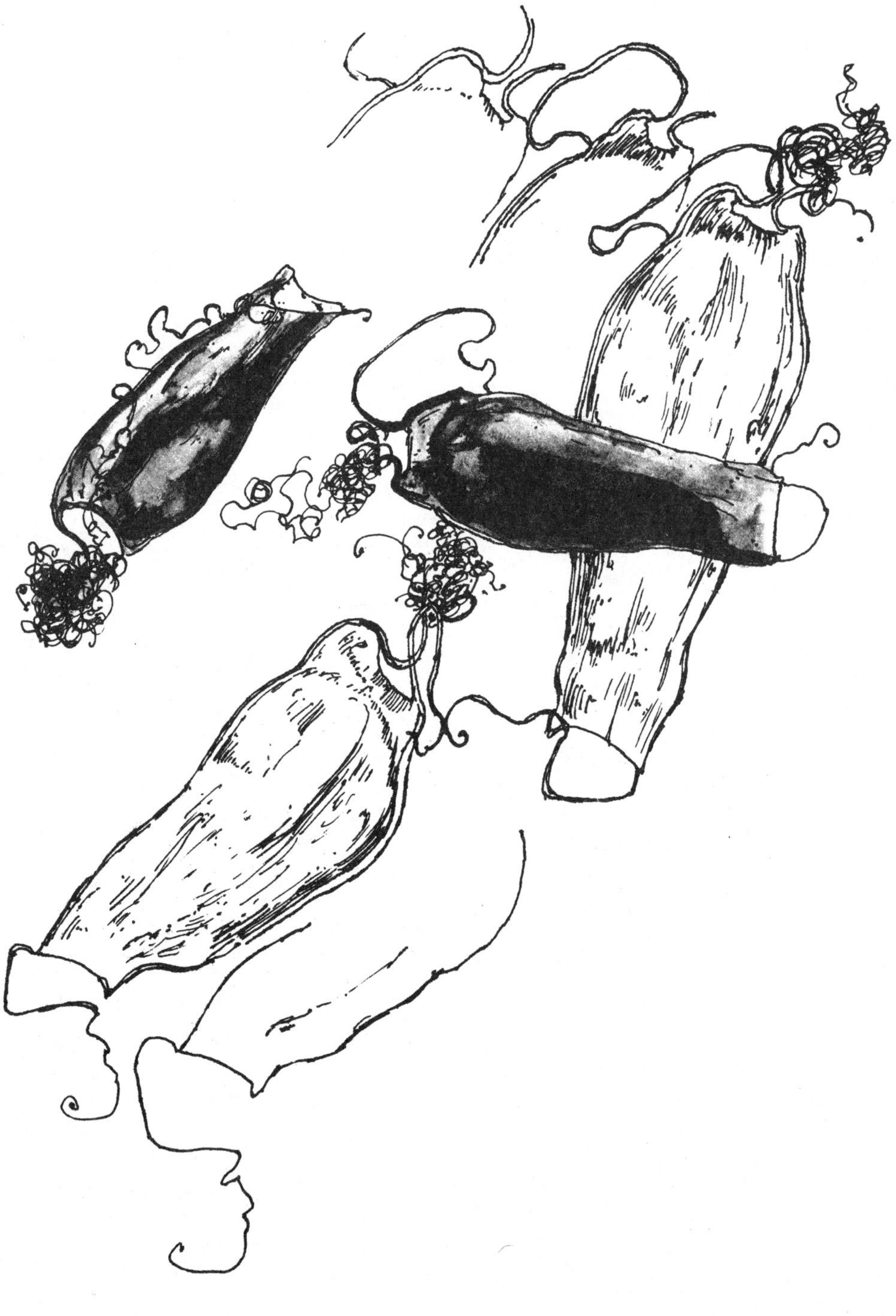

The spongey masses of dry bubbles often found on the shore are whelk eggs. They can be tackled in two ways. You can start with a group in the centre and work outwards. Or you can sketch the overall shape of the egg-mass and work inwards, using the more prominent and easily recognisable eggs as reference points.

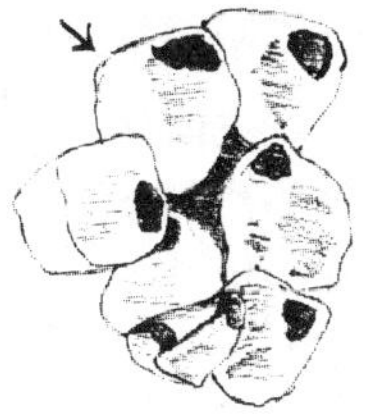

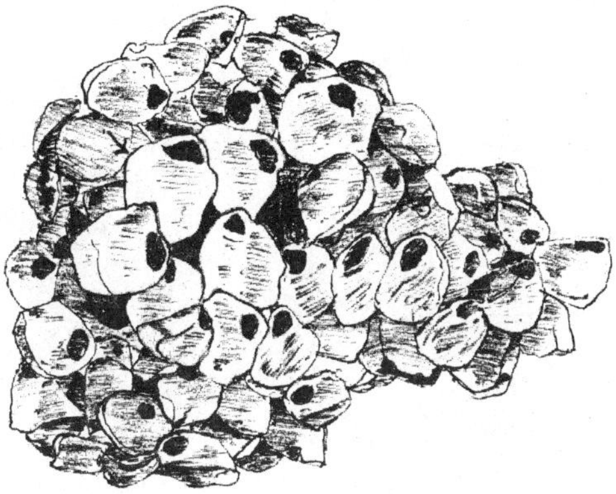

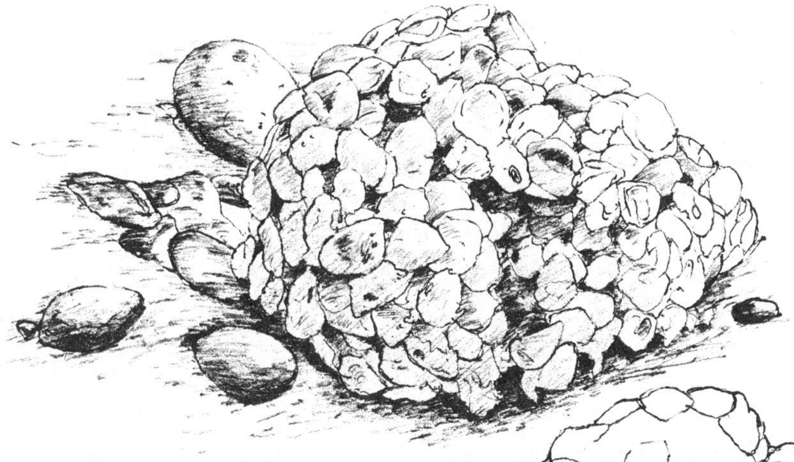

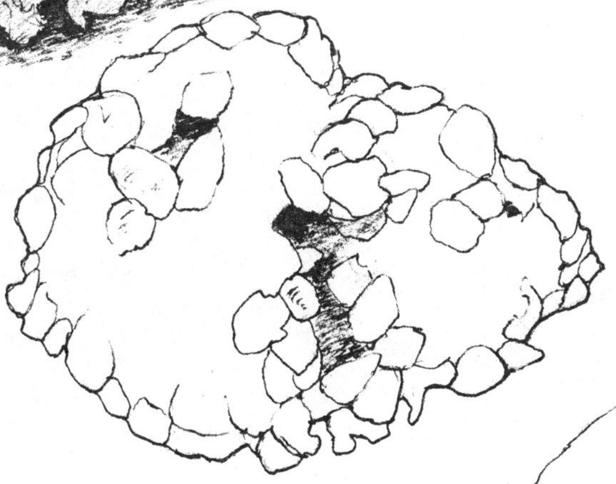

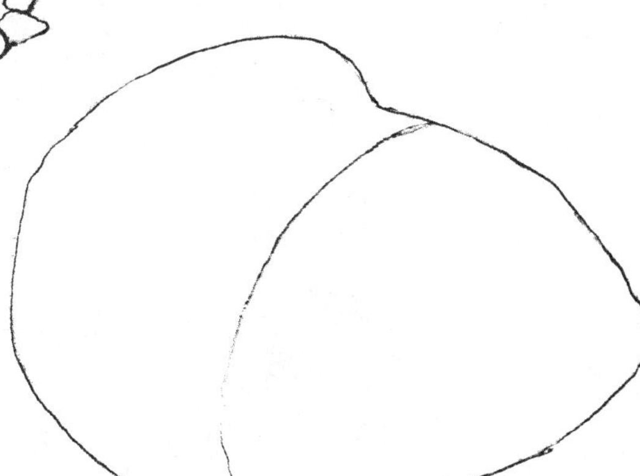

Bird and animal bones, weathered by sun and sea, have a fascinating intricacy and delicacy. In the drawing below I have combined a gull's skull with some feathers found nearby and a few stones. I used a B pencil which gave me the soft, whispy texture I needed for the feathers and yet could produce a fine hard line for the skull. By experimenting with different media you will soon discover which is most suited to a particular subject.

When drawing something as white as a skull, keep the area of bleached bone as white as possible, in contrast to the dark shading of the interior cavity. This whiteness is important for a convincing drawing — just as the earlier drawing of shags needed that dark wash to convey their blackness.

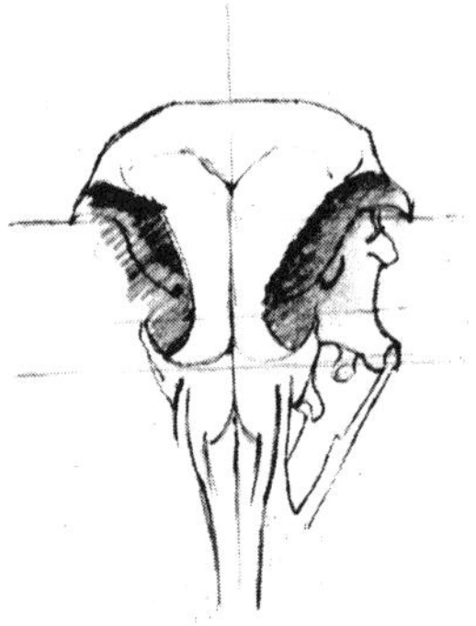

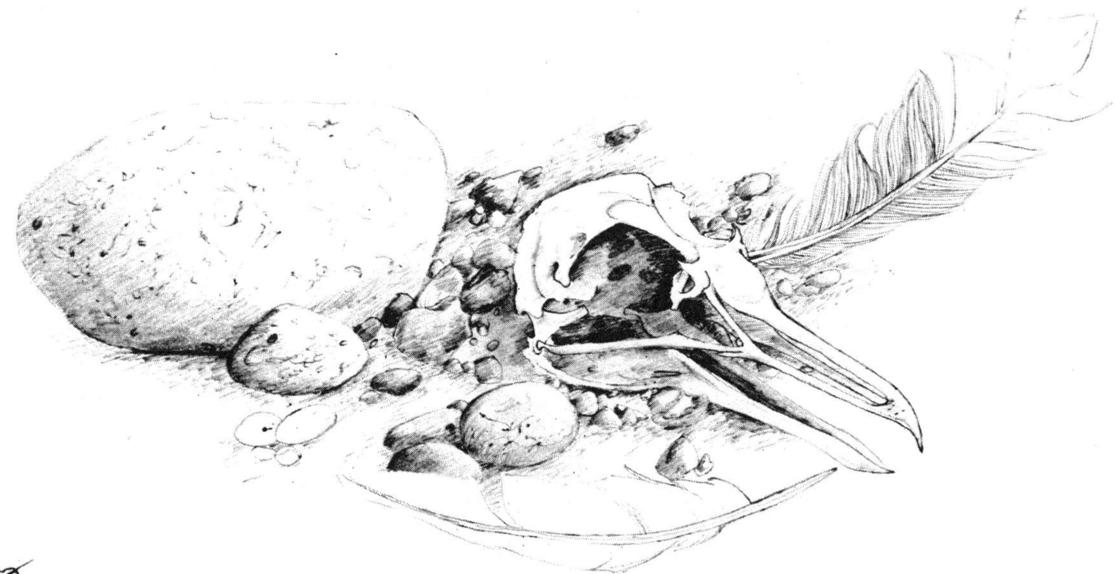

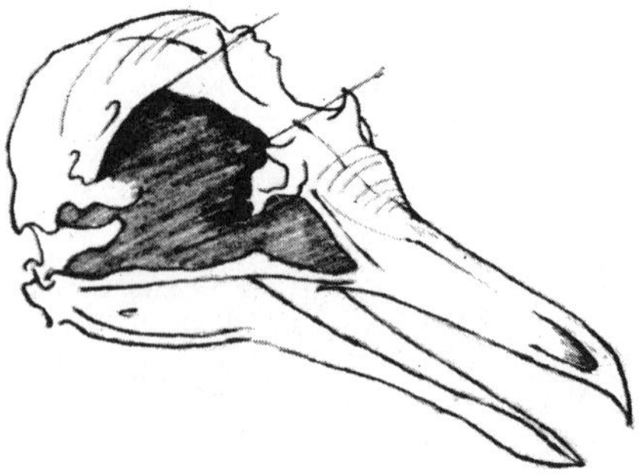

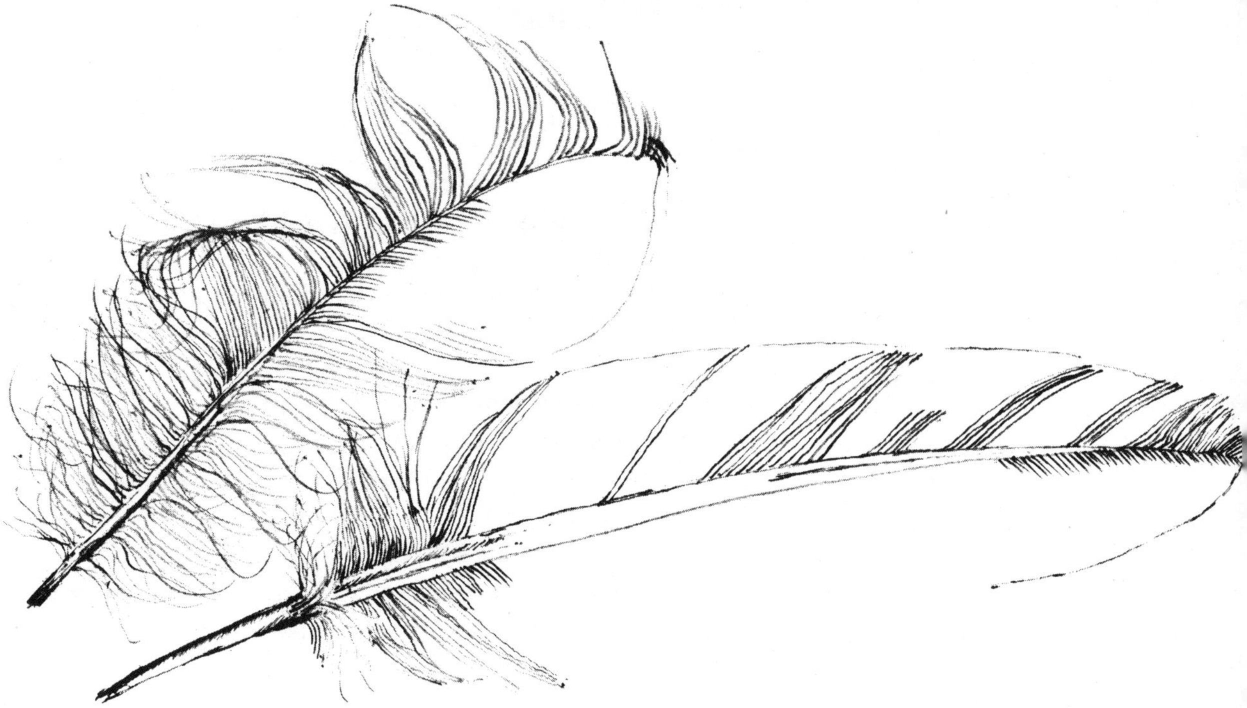

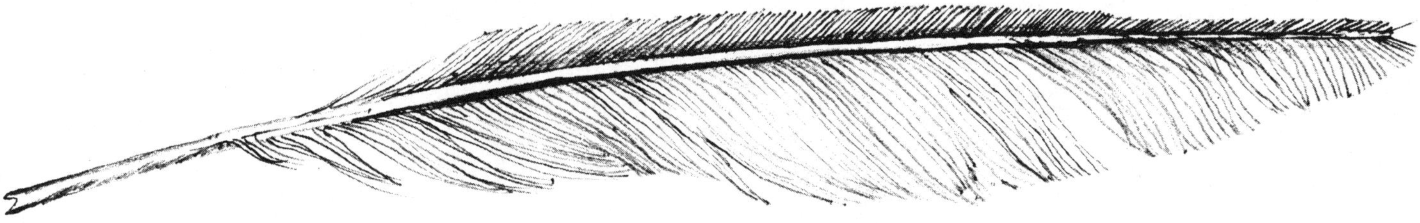

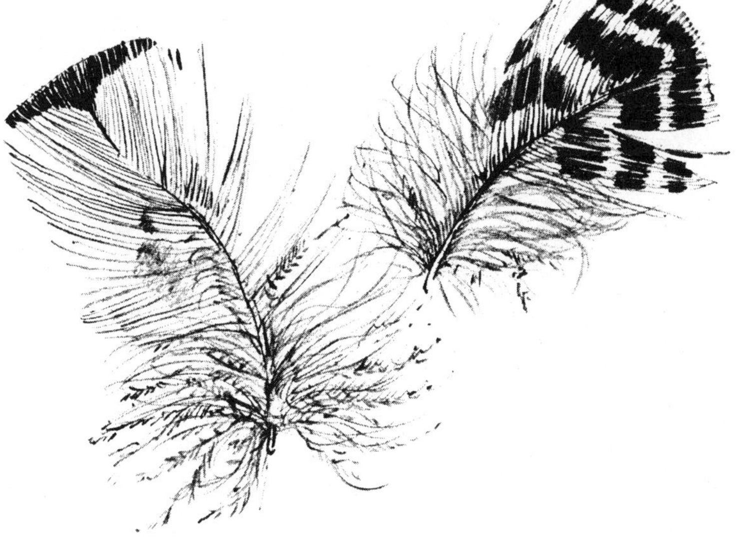

Notice that the structure of feathers varies. Breast feathers are soft and fluffy, wing and tail feathers much larger and stronger.

It is said that wherever man goes he leaves his mark, and the seashore is no exception.

It is a good idea to make some quick sketches of objects lying as you find them, before picking them up to take home. You can then refer to these on-the-spot sketches to add authenticity to your finished drawings.

For this composite drawing of sharp, hard, man-made objects found on the shore I chose a Gillott 303 pen. You could also try using a black ball-point for this kind of drawing — it produces an appropriately mechanical look.

Even a technically excellent drawing can look wrong if you have not observed your subject carefully before starting to draw.

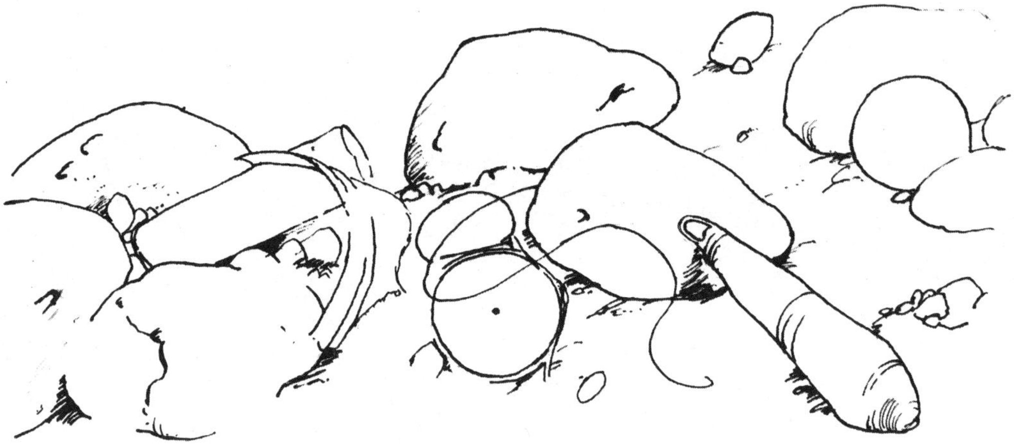

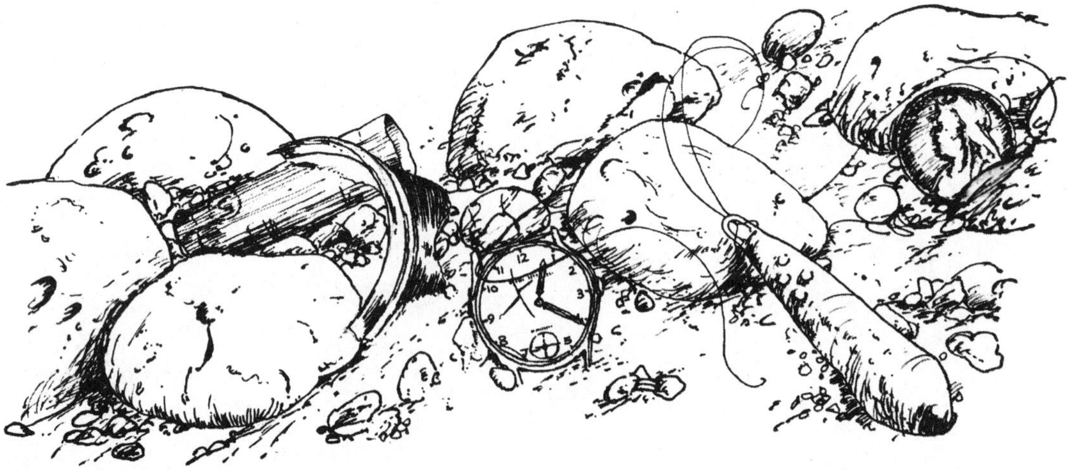

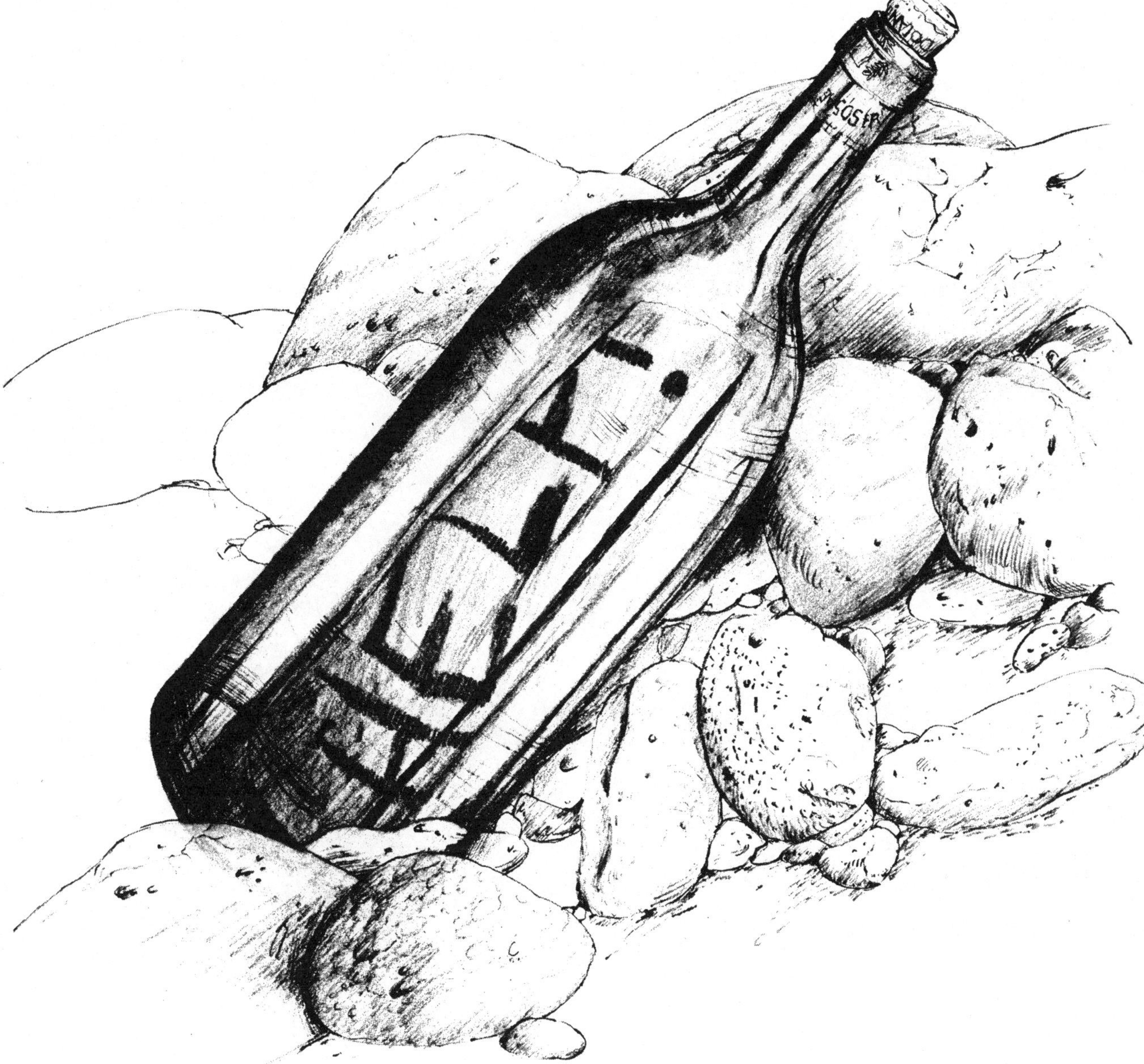

Water

Water is a reflecting surface and can therefore best be described by drawing the reflections in it. In bright sunny weather the sea sparkles with sharp spots of white reflected light.

In still water and pools the reflections will be almost unbroken; in this drawing of a redshank the broken line used for the reflection indicates the very slight movement on the surface.

In moving or disturbed water the reflection is broken up into fragments, as in the sketch of avocets, below.

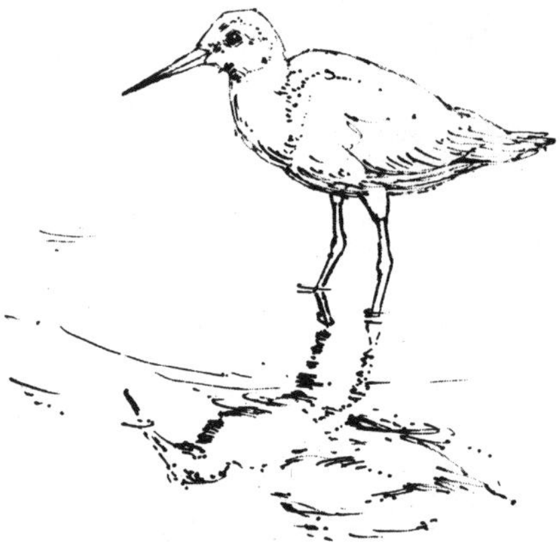

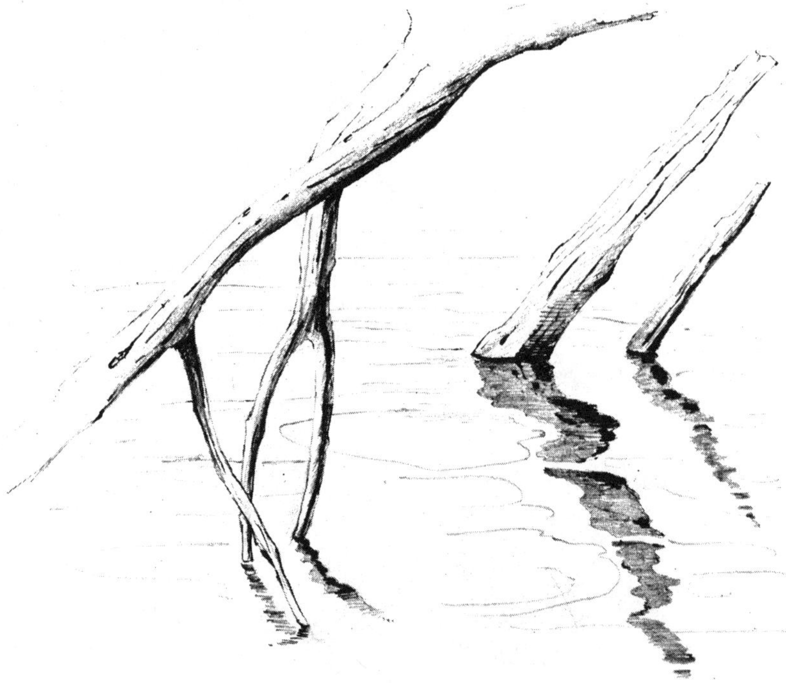

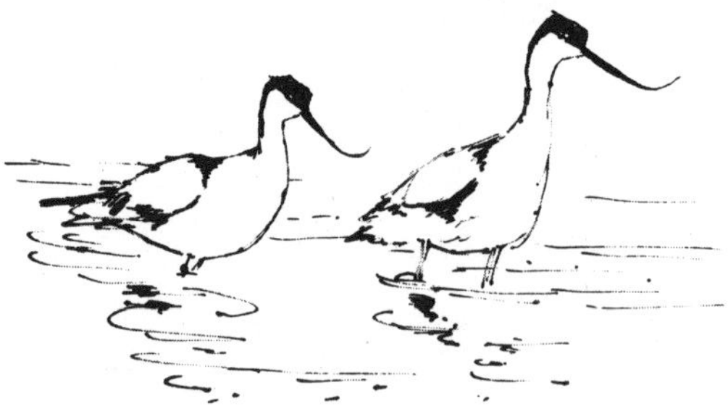

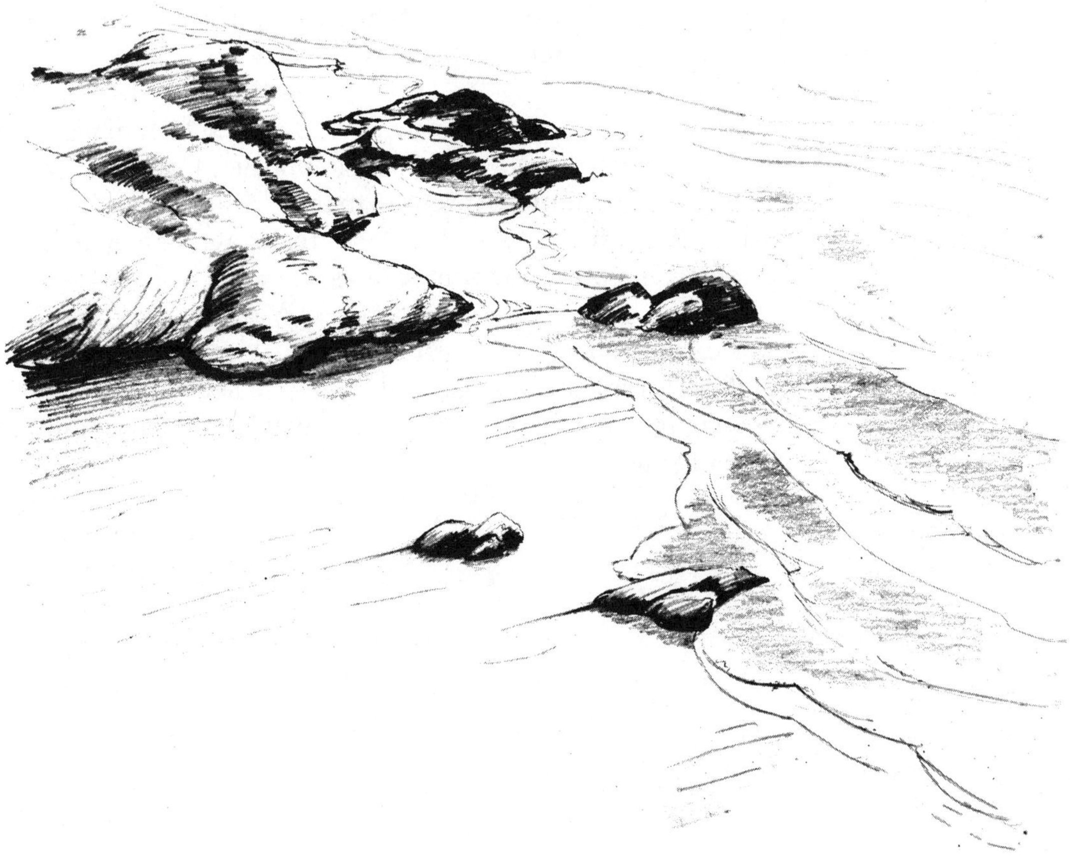

An area of wet sand on the edge of the sea will reflect very clear images, almost like a mirror, with sharp contrasts of light and shadow.

When drawing waves, remember the rules about perspective and receding horizontal lines. Notice that the edge of a breaking wave catches the light.

A few simple lines will convey the impression of water more effectively than any attempt at a detailed drawing. Use your line to indicate the direction of movement in the water.

The longer view

This book is concerned more with drawing the kinds of subject you can find on the seashore than with seascapes. But to give you an idea of how to tackle the longer view, here are three pen and ink sketches of different coastal views.

Don't be put off by the scale of the subject. Keep your sketches simple and forget about detail to begin with.

Remember that the further away any object is, the smaller and simpler it will appear. In the lower drawing opposite, I have drawn the rocks in the foreground more carefully than those further away, to indicate their solidity and texture. A distant breakwater or a boat out at sea can be conveyed with a few simple lines.

Look carefully at the proportions of sea, sky and land — it is easy to get these wrong and so distort the sense of space and distance. Adding a few figures or a boat in the distance will help to give your drawing a sense of scale.

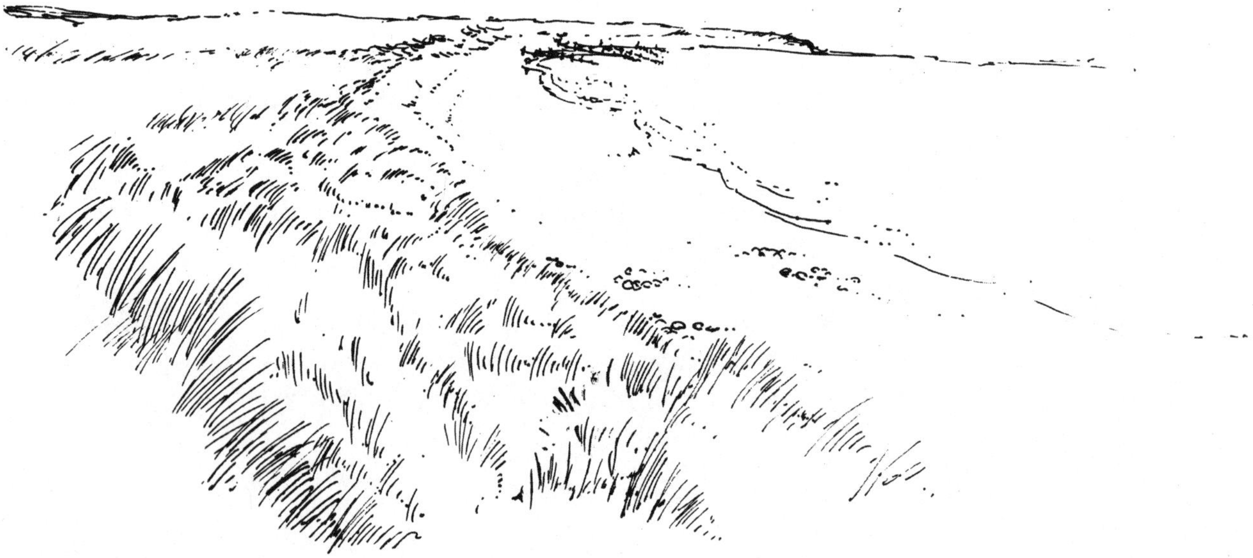

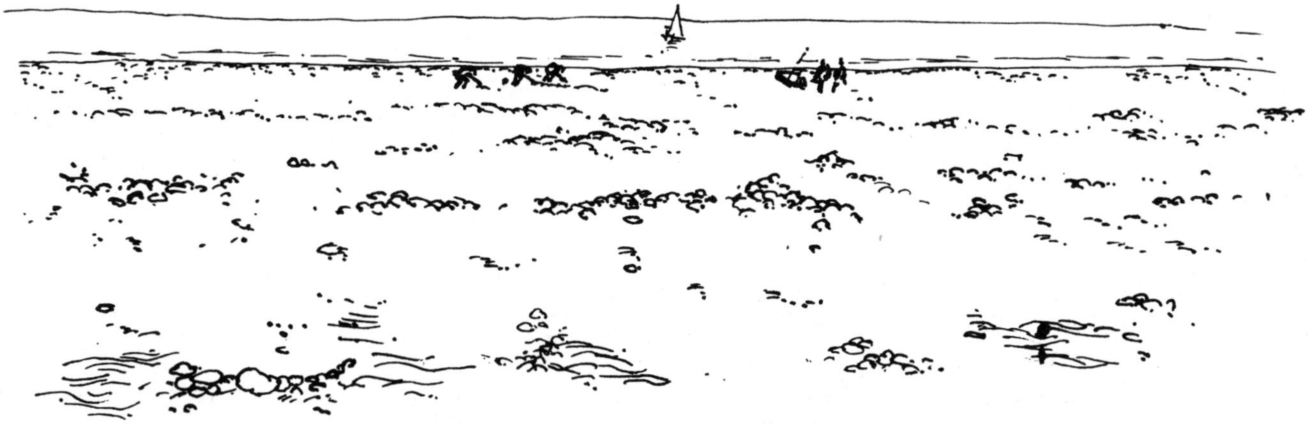

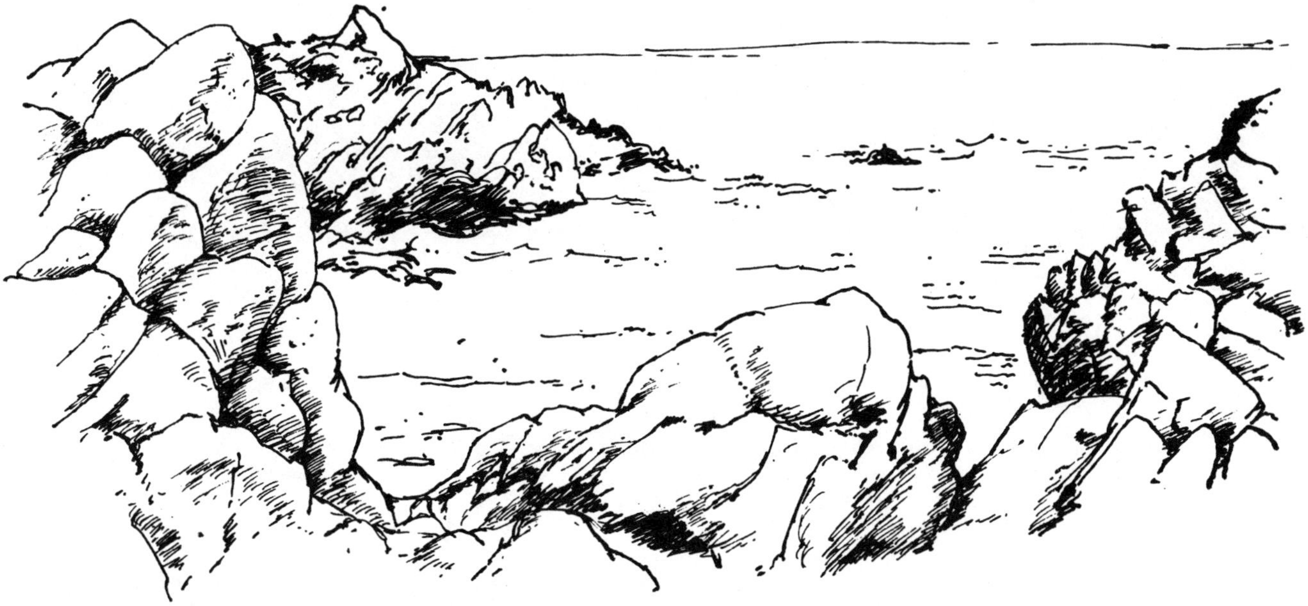

Finally, remember that rules are made to be broken. Every good artist is a good artist at least partly because of his originality — because he does what no one else has done before and because he breaks rules.

Every human being is unique. However poor an artist you think you are, you are different from everyone else and your drawing is an expression of your individuality. So be prepared to experiment — and enjoy yourself.

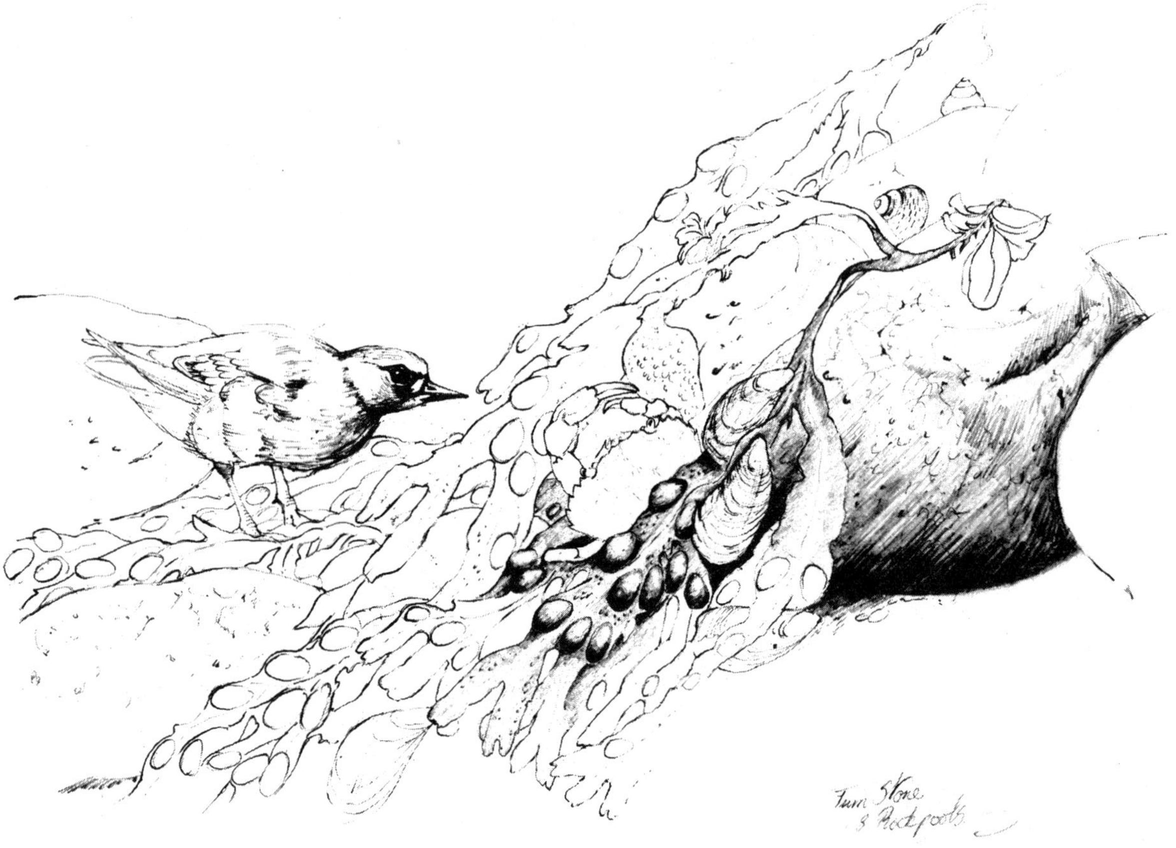